Lateral Marketing

Lateral Marketing

*New Techniques for Finding
Breakthrough Ideas*

PHILIP KOTLER
FERNANDO TRIAS DE BES

WILEY

John Wiley & Sons, Inc.

For general information on our other products and services please contact our Customer Care Department within the United States at (800) 762-2974, outside the United States at (317) 572-3993 or fax (317) 572-4002.

Wiley also publishes its books in a variety of electronic formats. Some content that appears in print may not be available in electronic books. For more information about Wiley products, visit our web site at www.wiley.com.

Designations used by companies to distinguish their products are often claimed by trademarks. In all instances where the author or publisher is aware of a claim, the product names appear in Initial Capital letters. Readers, however, should contact the appropriate companies for more complete information regarding trademarks and registration.

ISBN 0-471-45516-4

Printed in the United States of America.

10 9 8 7 6 5 4 3 2 1

*To Edward de Bono
and the other giants of creativity*

—Philip Kotler

*To the three women of my life:
Toya, my mother;
Maria del Mar, my wife;
and Blanca, my daughter*

—Fernando Trias de Bes

CONTENTS

vii

Contents

Contents

Contents

INTRODUCTION

Nowadays, a strikingly high percentage of new products are doomed to fail. Only 20 years ago, the proportion of failures to successes was much lower. Why is it so difficult to succeed with a new launch these days?

Let's examine the breadth of what's available today and what it means.

Take the cereal category, which features dozens of different subcategories and varieties, each addressed to a very specific target market: those who watch their weight, who need fiber for their digestion, who prefer cereal with fruit, who prefer cereal with chocolate, who prefer special-shaped cereals, and so on. Can there be any type of cereal not already found in the many current offerings?

In milk-based products, more than 50 varieties of

yogurts compete on the shelves of supermarkets. Among them are plain yogurts or with vanilla, those with pieces of fruit or with fruit blended in, low-fat or nonfat ones, and mousse variety. What further permutations are still possible?

In any developed country there are several dozen TV channels, whereas this number was under three or four 10 years ago. Is there room for more?

Today, only one out of every 10 sales promotions will obtain a response ratio higher than 5 percent, while some years ago this was the minimum you could expect with almost any promotion. Why is this happening?

Doing marketing today is not the same as it was in the 1960s and 1970s. Today there are products to satisfy almost every need. Customer needs are more than satisfied: They are hypersatisfied.

In the most developed markets, strategic fundamentals of marketing (i.e., segmentation, targeting, and positioning) are starting to show limitations as mechanisms for generating competitive advantages that can be translated into business opportunities and new products.

Companies can continue to segment the market more finely, but the end result is markets too small to serve profitably. Companies today need a new way of thinking about creating meaningful market offerings. We have reached a turning point in which marketing needs a new framework for generating ideas.

Recently, new business concepts have appeared that are the result of a different creative process than the endless vertical segmentation of yesterday.

- How was it possible to create the concept of cereal bars that would be eaten as a snack in the morning instead of having cereal with milk?[1]
- What creative process led to placing supermarkets at gas stations?[2]
- What mental process led to creating a refrigerated pizza that could substitute for a home pizza delivery service?[3]
- What mental process led to introducing a toy inside a chocolate candy?[4]
- Which idea generation system created the idea of a yogurt for active women to be taken to the office inside a bag, to be eaten in the middle of the morning?[5]

The most successful recent marketing ideas are based on a different paradigm than simply defining a market and endlessly segmenting it or repositioning it. The real breakthroughs stem from lateral thinking and a *lateral marketing* mind-set.

Our goal is to define a framework and theory for lateral marketing as opposed to vertical marketing. Edward de Bono, a worldwide authority on creative thinking, recommends thinking laterally as an ideal way to create ideas. We believe that lateral marketing thinking will provide more help to

---

[1]Examples: Hero Muesli cereal bars, Nutri-Grain bars.
[2]Examples: Mobil Marts, Cumberland Farms, Repsol shops (Repshops).
[3]Pizza Casa Tarradellas, Celeste.
[4]Kinder Surprise (Ferrero).
[5]Danio (Dannon).

companies, now that classical marketing thinking is not reaching the rates of success it achieved in the past.

We are not talking about discarding classical marketing thinking. Absolutely not. Current marketing theories are crucial. Our intention is to propose a broader vision about what marketing thinking can accomplish. Our aim is to expand the concept of marketing beyond the sequential and logical process on which it is based.

The idea is to incorporate lateral thinking as an additional platform for discovering new marketing ideas. The objective is to obtain ideas that consumers are not likely to request or propose to marketing researchers. These new ideas will help companies as they face growing product homogeneity and hypercompetition.

Lateral Marketing

The Evolution of Markets and the Dynamics of Competition

The last decades of the twentieth century were prosperous for most companies in the developed world. A stable period of peace, together with a strong demographic increase and a higher life expectancy contributed to this prosperity. To these factors we must also add the role of growing company marketing sophistication. Marketing departments had the use of large budgets to develop and launch new products, and educate and communicate with consumers toward generating product trial, repeat purchase, and brand loyalty.

But reaching success at the beginning of the twenty-first century is more difficult. Here are the main reasons.

1.1   In Consumer Packaged Goods, Distribution Concentration Has Increased Greatly

In the 1950s, distribution in the United States and Europe was largely in the hands of small independent retailers. Today, as a result of innovative distributors—companies like Wal-Mart and Ikea—and mergers and acquisitions, much distribution is in the hands of giant corporations and multinationals. Today, hypermarket and supermarket chains control (in the food sector) more than the 80 percent of final consumer purchases. And major franchises—McDonald's, KFC, Subway, Domino's Pizza—account for another major share. There are similar situations across all industries.

The bottom line is that power has been transferred from the manufacturers to the distributors. The distributors own the shelf space and decide which manufacturers to favor and how much shelf space to give them. They charge slotting fees and exit fees and virtually dictate the allowances and promotions they require.

Distributors respond by concentrating. Channels are concentrated in the hands of fewer distributors with a lot of power.

1.2 The Number of Competitors Has Been Reduced, but the Number of Brands Has Strongly Increased

Many producers were not able to survive the strong pressure of the giant retailers and either disappeared or were acquired by the "big fishes." Although there were now fewer producers, these producers continued to introduce more brands into the market. The following chart shows the growing number of registered brands in three countries between 1975 and 2000.[1]

---

[1]Source: World Intellectual Property Organization (WIPO). See www.wipo-org/ipstats/en.

Effective Registrations by Country of Origin

	United States	*United Kingdom*	*Germany*
1975	30,931	11,440	12,828
1995	85,557	33,400	21,934
2000	109,544	65,649	70,279

Three factors led to the increased number of brands:

1. First, there was the need to adapt products to the specific needs of certain groups of consumers (segments), and even to smaller groups (niches). This was established through the application of segmentation strategies.
2. Second, more brands make competitor attacks more difficult. It is harder to beat many brands all at once than to beat just the one that dominates a given category. Market atomization also discourages new competitors from entering the market.
3. Third, with more brands in the portfolio, the producer can negotiate better with the distributor. A higher discount offered on one brand compensates for a lower discount on another brand in the portfolio.

Multinationals and other corporations have been gaining in power. There are fewer players, but a higher number of brands.

1.3   Product Life Cycles Have Been Dramatically Shortened

New products last for a shorter time. Why?

In the first place, companies find it easier to launch new brands, especially if they have excess production capacity. They can introduce new ingredients, flavors, features, designs, or packaging with minimum changes in production processes. They can plan to absorb all the development costs in first-year sales and pray that the product can sell for a few more years.

In the second place, consumers increasingly are ready to try the new brands that they see advertised. They are willing to drop their previous brand if the new one is more satisfying. In turn, they may also drop the new brand if it fails to satisfy.

In the third place, consumer markets can be characterized as an arms race. Every new brand takes sales away from existing brands. Hurt competitors have no other way to recover than by also launching new brands. Other competitors then must retaliate with new brands, and on and on the cycle goes.

In the hypermarkets, the new brands take more shelf space, and as a result the desperate war for shelf space intensifies. The manufacturers move from brand management to category management to optimize the profitability of their scarce space.

Launching new brands is costing less. The dynamic of launching new brands is currently accelerated. New products survive in the market for shorter times.

1.4 It Is Cheaper to Replace than to Repair

Hard goods don't last as long as formerly. When they break down, it is easier to replace them with a later model than to repair them. Consider the following examples:

- A new laser printer costs around $180 and can be delivered in one day. Repairing it can cost nearly $120 and may take two weeks. Why would a consumer choose the old printer that may break down again?
- A new electric razor costs less than $60 and you can take it home immediately when you buy it. Repairing it can cost nearly $100 and may take two to three weeks. All shops recommend that you buy a new one.

It is often cheaper, faster, and easier, and saves you both money and time, to buy a new product than to repair it. The resulting culture is one that uses and accepts disposable products. Electrical appliances such as television sets or videotape recorders used to last seven or eight years, and now are replaced in two or three years. The acceptance of product disposability further fans the fever of new product launches.

Manufacturing processes are so efficient that replacing becomes cheaper than repairing. This accelerates the frenetic rhythm of new product launches.

1.5 Digital Technology Has Provoked a Revolution in Many Markets

Today everything can be transformed into zeros and ones: images, sounds, voice, text, and data. All are reproducible. Still pending is the ability to duplicate smell and flavor. It may be only a matter of time.

Digital technology has led to a whole new range of products: computers, interactive TVs, personal digital assistants, digital phones, smart dishwashers, microwaves, toasters, and so on. Technology is being extended to the most simple products: Books now come with sound and dolls are singing 20 melodies. Global Positioning Systems (GPS) are leading to a new set of satellite services such as locating stolen cars and missing people and animals.

And finally there is the Internet putting people in contact with millions of other people at almost zero cost. The Internet is still creating a revolution in the information, consumption, and communication practices of consumers; we are only at the beginning of this revolution.

The digital era facilitates the appearance of new products and services. Technology accelerates the rhythm of innovation and the number of new products. The Internet facilitates the appearance of new brands and ways of capturing business.

1.6   The Number of Trademarks and Patents Is Increasing

More new products are being developed to replace products that have been with us only a few years. As technology gets better, there are more upgrades to these new products. Applications, per year, to the U.S. Patent Office almost doubled during the 1990s.[2] It is getting difficult even to register trademarks with five or fewer letters since most of them have already been registered.

The growth in the number of patents and trademarks proves the increasing competitiveness of the markets.

1.7   The Number of Varieties of a Given Product Has Increased Radically

In any product category that you can name, you will find a greater number of varieties than in the past. Some examples:

- Go into a supermarket and write down the names of all the yogurts you can buy, by flavor and sizes. You can probably list over 50 different yogurts: plain, with sugar, with vanilla, with pieces of different fruits, various flavors, low-fat or nonfat, mousse, and so on.

- Look in any car magazine and count how many different types of vehicles and brands or variations are available:

---

[2] See John Grant, *After Image: Mind-Altering Marketing*, Chapter 2 (HarperCollins Publishers, 2002).

station wagons, minivans, SUVs, or small cars; diesel or no diesel; three, four, or five doors; different alternatives of engine power; and so on. In Spain, more than 450 models and brands can be bought at this moment.

- Take a look at the yellow pages and adult education brochures in your city and list all the types of hobby courses. Whereas some years ago the most frequent were courses in European languages, painting, dancing, music, and some sports, today you can find rarer interests such as tai chi, acupuncture, Japanese, Arabic languages, and hundreds of others.

Within a given category, the number of varieties available for consumer choice has increased exponentially. Categories are saturated with varieties.

1.8 Markets Are Hyperfragmented

Companies, in their search for differentiation, have identified and created more and more segments and niches, resulting in highly fragmented markets. Ultimately this will lead to one-to-one customized products and marketing. This makes it very difficult to find profitable market cells offering a promising return on investment. Additional volume will be incremental rather than substantial for every new product launched. The profits are shared until they are spread very thin.

Markets are fragmenting into small niches, which are less profitable.

1.9   Advertising Saturation Is Reaching Its Highest Levels, and the Fragmentation of Media Is Complicating the Launch of New Products

A normal citizen of a large urban area is daily exposed to an average of 2,000 advertising or communication stimuli. Out of these, only a few can be recalled at the end of the day. Advertising, once the most efficient way for brand building and the motor of new products penetration, is now threatened by its own growth, as proliferation of advertising is causing people to notice ads less.[3]

A brand manager launching a new chocolate bar today has real problems in communicating it effectively. Whereas several millions of consumers might have tried it some years ago when most people watched the same limited media, today's consumers may be watching any of 100 television stations, listening to any of 200 radio stations, or reading any of 1,000 magazines. If these consumers are not zapping the TV ads, they probably aren't watching TV at all and are instead spending their time at their computers or in outdoor sports or activities. Today's audiences are so diverse in their media habits that companies have to invest in many media to reach them. Advertising costs, as a result, may be too high.

---

[3]Jack Trout and Steve Rivkin proved this with interesting data: "At eighteen years old, a youth born in the UK has already been exposed to 140,000 TV ads. In Sweden, an average consumer receives nearly 3,000 daily commercial impacts. In 1994, the six TV channels of Madrid broadcasted 508,533 TV ads." See Jack Trout and Steve Rivkin, *The New Positioning: The Latest on the World's #1 Business Strategy* (New York: McGraw-Hill).

Advertising saturation is occurring.
Market segments are smaller and smaller.
Communicating a new product is getting more
expensive. It is necessary to be present with a
brand in many media to obtain good coverage.
This makes new product launches more expensive.

1.10 The Capacity of Obtaining Space in the Mind of the Consumer Has Been Reduced

From the previous discussion, one can understand how difficult it is to obtain space in the minds of the customers. It has the feel of a "Mission Impossible."

Consumers have become tremendously selective persons regarding products and advertising. They ignore most ads without having the feeling that they are losing anything important. Consumers have learned to look without seeing, to hear without listening.

Go to a doctor's office and observe someone in the waiting room looking through a magazine. Although exposed to more than 40 ads, that person probably isn't reading more than a few. Consumers need only half a second to pass by an ad.

The challenge is not only to fight against so many competitive products, brands, and ads, but also to fight against a closed consumer mind toward commercial communications. If your brand lacks novelty or special value, it will be ignored.

Claims that companies make about products such as "new," "improved," "better flavor," or "more natural" are strategies to capture the attention of customers. They are trying to promote novelty in order to fight against saturation.

Consumers have become selective. They are increasingly ignoring commercial communications. Novelty may be the only way to catch the attention.

Conclusion: Markets Are Much More Competitive

Doing marketing today is more complicated than ever. This is not to say that challenges did not exist in the past, but they certainly are different today. Now the challenge is to fight against fragmentation, saturation, and the storm of novelties that appear daily in the markets where we compete (see Figure 1.1).

And these thoughts bring us to an obvious and immediate conclusion: If (1) innovation and new products are the basis of competitive strategy, and (2) the rate of new product success is low, should it not be a high priority to find ways of creating and launching more successful products? In fact, this is one of the main objectives of *lateral marketing*.

We will start by analyzing how new products are conceived today. We will uncover this process in the second chapter.

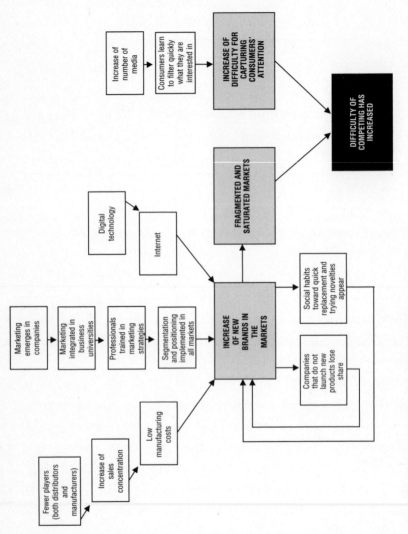

Figure 1.1 Marketing Overview

Summary

Innovation is the key and the basis of competitive strategies today. The rate of new product introductions is frenetic, but the failure rate is high. It is absolutely crucial to understand how innovation is done today. We need to split the marketing process into pieces and analyze it in order to understand the type of novelties it might produce.

Strengths and Weaknesses of Traditional Marketing Thinking

I n this chapter, we review the fundamentals of traditional marketing thinking and point out its strengths and weaknesses today. Understanding the difference between traditional and lateral marketing will be critical to implementing the complementary way of thinking.

2.1   Needs Identification as the Starting Point

Marketing starts by studying consumer needs and consists of knowing how to satisfy them. Yet many manufacturers forget to focus on needs and instead focus only on selling their products. Consider slide rule manufacturers. The slide rule is (was) a wood or plastic device on which many numbers were printed. Through gliding the parts of the rule, a user can carry out most arithmetic operations. In slide rules' heyday every engineer, as well as countless students, used one. But sales started to decline with the advent of the electronic calculator. The electronic calculator was faster, easier, and more accurate in producing numerical answers. Clearly, slide rule sales were falling because electronic calculators could meet the users' needs better.

Could the slide rule manufacturers have saved the slide rule by using the traditional strategies of segmentation, targeting, and positioning? Would it have helped to make separate slide rules for several different groups in different colors and by advertising that they feel good to hold and use? No!

Could the slide rule manufacturer have thought of a new product, such as electronic calculators, to substitute for slide rules? Segmentation thinking and positioning thinking would not have led to imagining an electronic calculator. The problem was a lateral problem, not a segmentation problem. Someone had to combine the idea of "slide rule" + "technology" + "a need to calculate" to create a new product that was more efficient than a slide rule.

Current marketing theories tend to work from the top down. They are not very effective in creating alternative or substitute products.

We will take yogurt as an example. Yogurt satisfies a set of needs: to allay hunger, to obtain calcium, to serve as a dessert or a snacking occasion, to be a self-reward, or to eat something healthy.

Because we see yogurt as satisfying hunger, we would not normally think that it might satisfy thirst, for example. We would not think of yogurt as competing with soft drinks. So, by starting with a particular need, we limit ourselves and fail to imagine "non-eating" needs that the product might serve.

> **Marketing starts by analyzing the need**
> **that products and services satisfy.**
> **Logically, identifying and selecting**
> **some needs implies discarding others.**

2.2   Market Definition

Once needs have been identified, the next step is determining who is in the market.

2.2.1   Selecting a Market

The market is defined as the persons or companies who have or may have the need we are intending to satisfy with the product or service that we sell.

We may want to add the situation in which the person will try to satisfy the need. The same person with a given need can, depending on the situation, behave in radically different ways.

For example, we can have a sugarless chewing gum in a weekday afternoon as a sweet, whereas on Saturday afternoon we might prefer an ice cream. We are exactly the same person but, depending on the situation, we behave differently. This leads to defining the market as *the set of persons/companies who buy or might buy products or use services in a given situation in order to cover a given need.*

> *The market is the set of current and potential persons/situations where the product can satisfy one or several needs.*

Going back to the yogurt example, we could define the current and potential market as any person older than one year old (approximate age when a child starts to eat yogurts) who is in a breakfast, dessert, or snacking occasion. This includes people of both genders, in any area of a given country.[1]

Advantage: The act of defining a market provides a very useful frame called the *target group*. The market definition is useful because it facilitates the development of the basic marketing strategies of segmentation and positioning.

Disadvantage: The market definition leads to thinking of persons/occasions that we can reach, but it excludes the nonpotential market. Going back to the yogurt example, with the previous market definition we are not going to consider babies younger than one year old.

> *The consideration and definition of a market provides a frame (an arena) where competing will take place. The act of selecting potential persons/situations leads to discarding persons/situations where the product will not be appropriate.*

---

[1]Only people allergic to milk-based products would be excluded. This group, given its small size, is not normally considered in the quantification.

2.2.2 Adoption of a Market Category and Subcategory by Marketers

When human beings think, they tend to use models.[2] A model is a set of elements integrated and put together in a set way. A model allows a great deal of information to be stored by codifying this information into a unity.

For instance, "coffee" is a model. It is a collection of elements: plant, bean, roast, water, heat, and cup. The word "coffee" is a shorthand.

The selection of concrete needs and persons/situations that our product or service can serve or satisfy is also a model—namely a market (see Figure 2.1).

And a market can be organized into categories and subcategories.

Here is an example.

1. *Need:* "to be informed regarding the world news about the economy."
2. *Persons:* "liberal professionals, executives, and businesspeople."
3. *Situation:* "first hour of the morning, weekdays."
4. *Product:* "newspapers."

The four elements are integrated to configure the category called "daily economy press" within the market of "information."

---

[2]See Edward de Bono, *Lateral Thinking: A Text Book of Creativity*, Chapter 19: "Concepts" (London: Pelican Books, 1970).

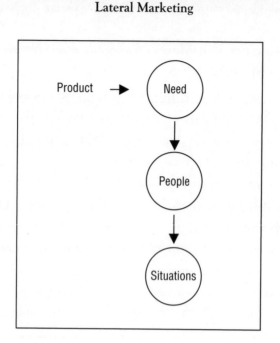

Figure 2.1   Market

All products and services marketed today in any country are included in a given category and, eventually, in subcategories. Ask any marketer to explain how the products of a given sector are structured or organized. He or she will draw a tree that will open categories and subcategories of different families of products.

These types of classifications are useful for five reasons:

1. They allow a given market to be quantified through enumeration of the products and brands that form part of it.

2. They allow the competitors to be listed.

3. They allow calculation of market share for each competitor in that category.

4. They allow the market volume to be tracked and the results of marketing actions to be evaluated.[3]

5. They provide a stable frame for the arena where we are competing.

Just collecting market data through distribution channels requires that all audited purchases be classified in a given category or subcategory. The problem is that once companies and marketing professionals adopt a category as a model, this will remain fixed and unaltered on an a priori basis.

The selection of the concrete needs and of the specific persons/situations where a product or service can be present constitutes a closed and complete system called category and subcategories.

Thus the milk-based market contains the yogurts category, which contains the yogurt with fruit subcategory, for instance.

Defining a category is necessary if we want to develop a marketing strategy, because we need to know where and against whom we are competing.

Fixing a market thus is helpful and yet has limitations.

---

[3]A. C. Nielsen, GfK, Taylor Nelson Sofres, and so on.

This conclusion is one of the most important ones of this book.

The consideration and definition of a market provides a frame of where to compete. The same act of selecting potential needs, persons, and situations leads to discarding the needs, persons, and situations where we cannot be present. When marketers adopt a category, they assume as fixed the elements within it (need, target, situation, and product). Normally, these elements will not be under consideration anymore.

We are not questioning or criticizing the main premises of marketing: needs identification and market definition. These two exercises are essential for developing a product's competitive strategy. We are, however, questioning the assumption that what we sell has a concrete utility applicable *only* to the people who require it.

2.2.3 Adopting a Market as Something Fixed Leads to Segmentation

Taking a market category as something fixed leads to segmentation as a unique way for opportunity seeking. If a category has been set, the only way to find new arenas is by selecting some subgroups of customers within that category.

Segmentation and positioning rely on the assumption of a

market that cannot be altered.[4] This means that the only way to find new opportunities is by redefining a market, changing its elements.

The definition of a market inevitably leads to segmentation and positioning strategies. Defining a market leaves only one option to compete: to fragment the market into parts. This is the essence of the segmentation strategy.

2.3   Segmentation and Positioning as Competitive Strategies

Segmentation and positioning have proved to be the two most relevant strategies in traditional marketing. We will highlight their advantages and limitations as generators of competitive advantages in the long term.

2.3.1   *Segmentation*

Imagine that we are in the first years when yogurts started to be produced commercially. Normally, markets are born with a first brand that creates the category.

There is a current and potential market for the category,

---

[4]We are mainly referring to business operational segmentations (fixed market). It is always possible to define an exploratory-type segmentation (extended market), the latter of which might lead to some lateral ideas. Nevertheless, day-to-day marketing together with the implementation and control marketing programs of companies force marketers to work with operational segmentations (fixed market) most of the time. We can call this market myopia.

represented by the rectangle in Figure 2.2. And the first brand is represented by the point inside it.

If there is enough volume, another competitor is likely to appear if it senses a good opportunity. The result is Figure 2.3.

Let's imagine that a third competitor appears. It may encounter difficulties since the first two players normally occupy substantial parts of the market. Very frequently the first two brands in any market grab 75 percent of the pie leaving little space for new competitors.

What then can be done? Since you won't be the leader, choose a subgroup of persons/situations in the market and ad-

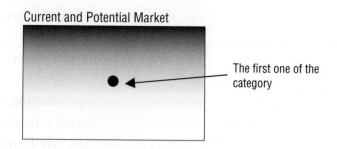

Figure 2.2   The First Brand Creates the Category

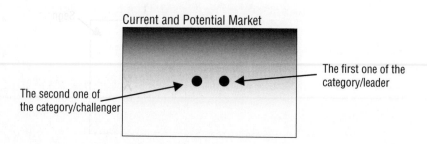

Figure 2.3   Challenge by the Second Brand

dress your product directly to them. Identify important aspects of these persons/situations and communicate these aspects in your product proposition.

In summary, segmentation tells us: "Renounce attacking the whole market. Show yourself as the most efficient option for a subset of the market and you can become the leader of that segment. It is better to be the head of the mouse than the tail of the lion."

So this third competitor cuts or segments the market to create a part that highlights a concrete characteristic of the product. This characteristic determines your positioning (see Figure 2.4).

Positioning consists of choosing how we want to be perceived. We are telling a part of our market: "I am different because I have these characteristics; and if these are the ones that you consider important, the ones that you prefer, I am the best option for you."

The advantage of a segmentation and positioning strategy is obvious: to divide and conquer. Whereas following an undifferentiated strategy (i.e., to attack the whole market

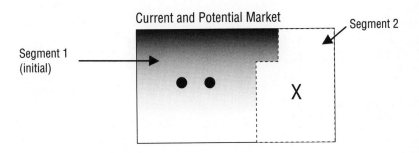

Figure 2.4   Segmentation

without segmenting it) we obtain only some market share, by segmenting the market we obtain the major share of that segment.

Segmentation and positioning provide an additional advantage: Since certain groups of customers find their needs better covered, they will increase their consumption—will eat more yogurt, for example. So segmentation provokes a double effect: It fragments the market and at the same time makes it bigger.

When a market is first segmented, the effect is positive for the segmenter. But as segmentation increases, the segments get smaller and less profitable. Furthermore, some competitors don't carve out new segments but start invading existing segments (see Figure 2.5).

Eventually the competitive dynamics lead to the market looking like Figure 2.6.

Figure 2.6 describes very well the situation of a good part of the American and European markets in those categories that are in a mature phase. Now we can illustrate the immediate and long-term effects of a segmentation strategy.

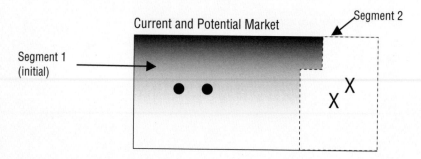

Figure 2.5   Invading Existing Segment

Current and Potential Market—Fully Segmented

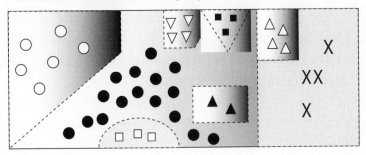

Figure 2.6   Fully Segmented Market

Immediate effects: Segmentation allows the generation of competitive advantages to any new competitor that enters the market.

It also allows the market leader to create barriers to competition. Each year Dannon (Danone) launches many new yogurt varieties in the European market. In most European countries Dannon (Danone) has a market share over 80 percent and still continues segmenting. In this way, it discourages the entry of new competitors.

We also noted that segmentation helps to increase the size of the market.[5] It makes products more attractive to certain groups of consumers, increases their consumption frequency, and facilitates the conversion of potential customers into current customers.

Long-term effects: Repeated segmentation leads to hyperfragmentation of markets. Segments are converted into

---

[5]Note that Figures 2.4 to 2.6 each show a bigger square, representing a market whose volume is growing.

niches and eventually we start talking about one-to-one marketing. Hyperfragmented and saturated markets reduce success ratios of new products and brands. Marketing is in desperate need of new alternatives to segmentation for generating profitable businesses.

Segmentation consists of dividing the market to obtain new sales. Segmentation can increase the size of the market as well. Repeated use of segmentation finally fragments and saturates the markets. Market fragmentation leaves little room for new products. But new products are key components for companies that want to grow.

2.3.2 Positioning as a Strategy for Generating Competitive Advantages

Positioning is linked to the act of segmenting. We showed earlier that positioning consists of highlighting some characteristics of our product in order to differentiate it from competitors' products. Positioning can work to target a new segment, and it allows differentiation within a given segment.

In Figure 2.6, each brand has or seeks a concrete positioning,[6] even the ones within the same segment. In

---

[6]Almost all marketing strategies for differentiation consist of selecting functional, existential, or symbolic attributes.

the case of yogurt, there are brands positioned as healthier, cheaper, fresher, or more natural. Even in the low-fat yogurt subcategory, we find brands that have "less cholesterol" and ones that have "better flavor." Choosing a characteristic and accentuating it give personality to our brand, make it different from the rest, and make it more noticeable.

Immediate effects: Positioning strategy creates differentiated brand personalities even within the same market. Often it defines the brand by a single word: Volvo is safety, BMW is sportiness and driving performance, Mercedes-Benz is luxury. Positioning allows a brand to be positioned differently in different markets. For example, the same Volvo whose safety is emphasized in the United States is positioned as a durable car in the Mexican market. Heineken is a status beer in the United States and a grocery beer in Belgium.

Long-term effects: Positioning opens up even more possibilities than the number of brands, because the same brand may be positioned differently in different markets. It adds to the number of perceived varieties in the market. At the same time, marketers tend to position with logical, functional, symbolic, and experiential aspects of products and ignore other possibilities. For example, although it doesn't make sense to say that a yogurt is "fast," we might show that some illogical characteristics can germinate new product ideas.

Positioning consists of choosing something by which we want to be recognized. Positioning, as a strategy, opens further opportunities for variation. Positioning consists of choosing characteristics and highlighting them. Selecting logical characteristics of our products may blind us to innovative new concepts.

2.4   The Development of the Marketing Mix: The Only Thing That Is Seen

The exercise of segmentation, targeting, and positioning is followed by the practical fleshing out of the marketing mix, known as the 4Ps: product, price, place, and promotion. This is the tangible embodiment of the marketing strategy. When we say that the marketing mix needs coherence, we mean that not only must the mix elements be consistent with each other but also they must be derived from and consistent with the segmentation and positioning strategies.

The marketing mixes are the operations where 90 percent of marketing management effort goes. Most marketing professionals' time, resources, and budgets are dedicated to the marketing mix formulation, implementation, and control.

Given that the marketing mix is to be derived from segmentation and positioning thinking, we conclude that marketing mixes suffer from the limitations alluded to earlier in segmentation and positioning thinking. The result is that new products generate less incremental volume, are more vulnerable to more cannibalization, and achieve less suc-

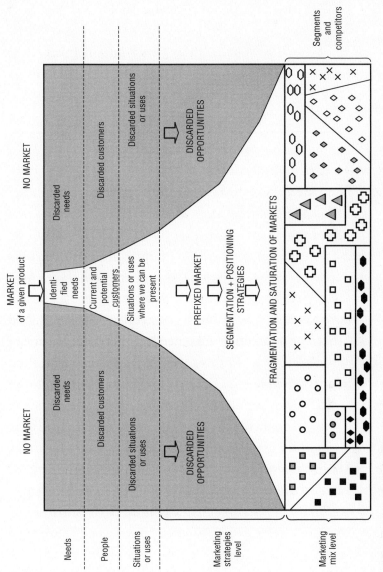

Figure 2.7 Marketing Process

35

cess in today's marketplace. The new products that result from segmentation and positioning will be described in Chapter 3.

Summary

The marketing process is a sequence (see Figure 2.7). It starts with needs identification in order to establish the persons/situations that become our potential market. The market such as it is defined is considered fixed and stable. Using a prefixed market allows the establishment of a competitive frame and allows tracking of key performance indicators about that market (or category): size, variation, market share. Defining a market is the basis of the segmentation, targeting, and positioning strategies and ultimately of the definition of the marketing mix. In fact, an operational segmentation is possible only because a context named market has been defined. Repeated segmentation leads to hyperfragmentation of markets, which reduces the chances of innovating successful new products. To visualize a market as a fixed model is extremely useful, but at the same time it blinds us to other innovative possibilities. This can constitute a loss of opportunities.

Innovations Originated from Inside a Given Market: The Most Common Way of Creating Innovations

In the preceding chapter, we reached the following conclusions:

- The marketing process is a sequential process.
- It centers on needs and trying to satisfy them with appropriate offerings.
- The aim of marketers is to define and quantify the set of persons/situations with these needs. This grouping is called the potential and current market. The identification of this target ultimately leads to the development of marketing strategies.
- Marketing strategy development relies on segmenting the current and potential market, together with searching for differentiating attributes for positioning brands and businesses.
- The application of segmentation and positioning used repeatedly by many companies leads to market saturation and hyperfragmentation, regardless of the size increases that it provokes.

- In the long term, the fragmentation effect overwhelms the expansion effect and reduces the likely success of new products within that market.

Working from the market definition downward leads to new products that are just variations of existing products and services.

Do the following exercise: Go to any supermarket and look at the section containing breakfast cereals. You will find normal cereals, with and without sugar, toasted, with chocolate, with bran, with fiber, with fruits, with nuts, in single size or family size, and many others.

Now browse the other sections of the supermarket. You will likely not find any other products incorporating cereals. Don't cereals have other applications such as candy bars? The habitual tendency of companies is to assume the market is a fixed starting point with the result that most new ideas form within the existing category.

Here are the major approaches to developing new products based on assuming the market is fixed.

3.1 Innovations Based on Modulation

Modulation-based innovations consist of variations in any basic characteristic of a given product or service, by increasing or decreasing that characteristic. We are mainly referring to functional or physical characteristics. Here are some examples of innovations based on modulations:

- *Juices:* with low sugar content, with more fruit, not from concentrate, with vitamins, without additives.
- *Detergents:* with more bleach, with more soap concentration, with more perfume, fragrance free, with more foam, with less residue.
- *Banking:* with monthly interest payment, without charges for credit card usage, with a higher number of offices, with better trained staff.
- *Couriers:* faster delivery, higher maximum weight, extended payment terms, higher frequency of deliveries, higher guarantees in case of loss or product stolen.

A constant in all these modulations is that an essential product characteristic is accentuated or decreased.

These policies are ideal for segmenting markets because they allow the offer to be adapted more efficiently to some parts of the current and potential market. These policies better impact certain targets and, in parallel, increase the size of the markets.

Modulation-based innovations vary any basic characteristic of the product or service by increasing or reducing the weight, importance, or degree of that characteristic.

41

3.2   Innovations Based on Sizing

Sizing-based innovations launch a new product onto the market by varying its volume without changing anything else.
Some examples:

- *Soft drinks:* 10 ounces, 20 ounces, one liter, two liters, six-packs of 10-ounce bottles (60 ounces total).
- *Potato chips:* 5-ounce bag, 12 ounces, 20 ounces, multi-packs that contain several bags for family consumption, and so on.
- *Internet connection service:* bonus of 30 minutes per day, 60 minutes per day, 90 minutes per day, two hours per day, five hours per day, flat-rate tariffs without usage limitations.
- *Production machines repair service:* one hour per week contract, two hours per week, five hours per week, daily review contracts.
- *Advertising agencies:* full service limited to either creative, media purchasing, packaging designs, sales promotion, or sponsorship.
- *Nonprofit organizations:* different levels of donation: $6 per month, $12 per month, $30 per month, $60 per month.

In these cases the product or service never changes. The only thing that changes is the intensity, the frequency, the number, or the volume of the offer.

An advantage of these policies is that they allow the possible number of consumption or usage occasions to be increased. For example, different sizes of soft drinks allow individual buying for immediate consumption or family consumption or home product storing.

Another advantage is that by offering different sizes it is easier to extend consumption or usage to the maximum number of potential customers, since we adapt the offer to the different volumes required by every customer depending on every individual situation or family size.

Many companies have observed that by launching a new size of a product, total sales of the new format are always higher than the reduction of the existing ones. Cannibalization occurs but total volume increases. So, sizing-based innovations are good since they develop markets by facilitating the conversion of potential into current customers.

Sizing-based innovations consist of introducing a new product or service in the market by varying the volume, frequency, size, or number of products or services offered.

3.3 Packaging-Based Innovations

The way a product is packaged can modify the perceived benefit, function, or consumption occasion of the product or service. Here are some examples:

- *Chocolates:* Nestlé markets the brand Red Box chocolates in different types of boxes, although the flavors and shapes of the chocolates are always the same. One container is a small, simple paper-made box sold in impulse channels such as kiosks or candy shops. The function of the product is to satisfy a whim or provide a snack.

A much bigger paper-made box is marketed in supermarkets and hypermarkets, and its function is family consumption at home.

There are also chocolates in a round metal tin sold in pastry shops that functions as a gift.

There is a container of even higher quality consisting of the same metal box, but decorated with drawings by the architect Antoni Gaudí. This is a premium container ideal as a gift on very special occasions.

- *Banks:* In services, the container could be the environment where the service is provided. For example, banks have different brands oriented to different target markets expressed through the offices' layouts and decorative styles. There are banks for high-level customers, middle classes, young depositors, and so on.

- *Butane gas:* In the energy sector, different types of containers allow extending the industrial use of, for example, butane gas to different industries or individuals. Butane gas in canisters is ideal for gas consumption in houses. The gas bottled in square metal containers has been used by taxi drivers as a fuel. Distribution of butane gas in trucks has allowed small manufacturers to use it for production purposes. Butane gas in small amounts is used in lamps for camping or similar applications.

The interesting thing about packaging/container-based innovations is that the product is absolutely the same, but an adaptation of the container allows not only volume variation (related to sizing-based innovations), but also being present in a higher number of situations and occasions. This facilitates reaching and serving more customers and developing a market to its maximum potential.

Packaging-based innovations consist of creating new products by modifying only the container, the packaging, or the environment. Many times, packaging changes can be made together with sizing changes.

3.4 Design-Based Innovations

Design-based innovations are those where the product, the container or package, and the size sold are the same, but the design or look is modified. Here are examples:

- *Cars:* A car company will launch the same product with a different exterior design. There is little differentiation between a Buick and a Pontiac except for styling differences. Few people know that minivans are pickups with a design adaptation of the car body.
- *Skis:* Many ski manufacturers innovate from one year to another just by changing design and colors. Manufacturing materials of skis change mainly in the most expensive models. In the rest, just a good restyling ensures purchase interest.

- *Watches:* When Swatch introduced the modern new Swiss watches collection, design became the main source of innovation. Swatch is introducing new models each year, but external appearance is the main change.

Design-based innovations expand the targets for a given product or service by attracting buyers who respond to new styles and different positioning.

Design-based innovations are those which create a new product by changing its external appearance.

3.5   Innovations Based on Complements Development

A salad can be different every day by adding carrots, olives, boiled egg, onion, cheese, and so on. Innovations based on complements development involve adding some ingredient to the basic product to permit variety creation. Here are examples:

- *Cookies:* Cookies with sugar sprinkled on them, with cinnamon, with milk chocolate, with white chocolate, with dark chocolate, filled cookies, cookies with cream, with coconut, with butter.
- *Hand soap:* Soap with moisturizers, with coconut aroma, with floral aroma, antibacterial soap.
- *Moving services:* Services for helping people move from one house to a new one can add ingredients to the basic

service: arranging clothes in closets, furniture storage while the house is being painted, special systems for fragile objects.

- *Computer assistance services:* In the industrial sector, companies can offer various complements. A computer service company can offer maintenance, ink toner replacement, computer or printer replacement while being repaired, antivirus programs.

Innovations based on complements usually are announced as follows: "Now with . . . !" These policies can create a positive effect in the mature phase of a product by introducing a variation on a theme to rekindle interest in the product.

Innovations based on complements consist of adding complementary ingredients or additional services to the basic product or service.

3.6   Innovations Based on Effort Reduction

Whenever we buy a product or service, we exert an effort and there is a cost. There is a cost in the money we pay, the time dedicated to complete the purchase process, the risks we take with our decision, and the associated costs in the postpurchase period, such as repairing or maintaining hard goods that we buy. We can innovate by helping to reduce the customers' efforts and costs. Some examples:

- Charles Schwab helps people buy and sell equities at a discount. The firm recognizes that people prefer different channels for doing this. So it has set up offices, telephone ordering lines, and online ordering in order to give the customer whatever level of effort he or she wants to use to carry on transactions.
- Fnac, the French distributor of books, records, videos, and computers, reduced the customer perception of the risk of making a wrong decision. The policy consisted of stamping all prices in the store with the message "Minimum price guaranteed." Fnac commits to paying the price difference if you find the same product in any other shop at a lower price. Fnac is removing your need to make a special effort to go elsewhere to find better prices because it stands for the lowest prices. Otherwise many consumers would be claiming their money!

A firm known for its expensive perfumes decided to introduce mass market perfumes in attractive bottles at much lower prices. Through the effort reduction of lower prices, the firm converted an enormous mass of potential buyers into current buyers.

Innovations based on effort reduction do not modify the product or service but increase the size of the market. They increase value by reducing the denominator in the value equation rather than increasing the numerator:

$$\text{Value} = \frac{\text{Benefit}}{\text{Effort}}$$

$$\uparrow \text{Value} = \frac{\text{Benefit}}{\downarrow \text{Effort}}$$

Innovations based on effort reduction consist of modifying not the product or service, but rather the efforts and risks involved in the purchase.

Summary

The policies we have explained are summarized in Table 3.1. All these innovations have a common factor:

These innovations consist of continued variations on what the product or service is, but do not intend to modify its essence. The innovations occur within the category in which they compete, since the methodologies for creating them assume a fixed market.

Why is this observation so important? Because these innovation strategies *are the most habitual ones and they do not change the basic product.*

Table 3.1 Approaches to New Product Development

Type of Innovation	Consists Of	Effect in the Market
Based on modulation	Increasing or decreasing any characteristics of the product or service	• Amplification of targets • Ability to better serve concrete segments
Based on sizing	Variations of volume, quantity, or frequency	• Amplification of targets • Amplification of consumption occasions
Based on packaging	Modifications of container or packaging	• Amplification of targets • Amplification of consumption occasions
Based on design	Modifications of design in order to communicate different lifestyles	• Amplification of targets • Differentiation by lifestyle
Based on complements	Adding ingredients or complementing/ adding additional services	• Ability to better serve concrete segments or niches • Increase in the range of products
Based on effort reduction	Reduction of the efforts customers make in the purchase process	• Conversion of potential buyers into current buyers • Ability to reach the maximum penetration of the product or service

It is true that these innovations have very positive effects, since they can increase the size of the market and facilitate conversion of potential consumers/situations into current ones.

But **these innovation policies do not create new categories or new markets. The innovation always occurs within the category where the idea originated.**

For example, if we advertise cheese with 0 percent cholesterol, we are now able to sell cheese to a new segment, "cheese lovers worried about their weight and cholesterol." But as segmentation is repeatedly applied by competitors as their form of innovation, the market becomes hyperfragmented and saturated. Figure 3.1 shows the structure of many categories of products after the six strategies of innovation are continuously applied.

Figure 3.2 shows a soft drink example.

The most basic marketing strategies—segmentation and innovation—are in a crisis. Marketers are obliged to increase sales and market share in markets and categories that are saturated.

In recent years, however, we have observed companies that are applying another way of thinking. They are discovering original new offerings that yield much higher returns than the ones originated by innovating within a given market.

Chapter 4 is dedicated to explaining and illustrating this new way of thinking.

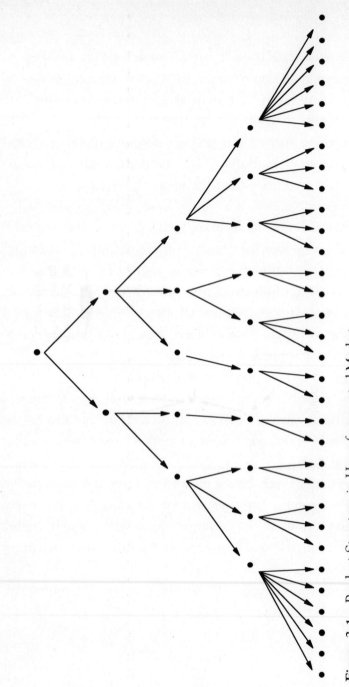

Figure 3.1 Product Structure in Hyperfragmented Market

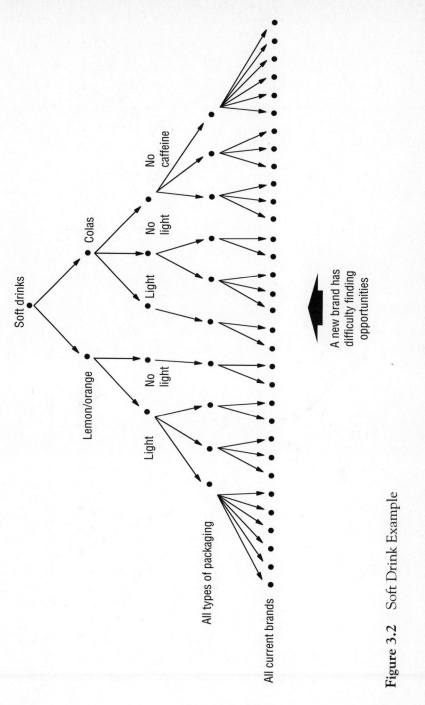

Figure 3.2 Soft Drink Example

53

Innovations Originated Outside of a Given Market: An Alternative Way to Create Innovation

T his chapter describes cases where companies have used a different process for searching for and creating new ideas. The method is called *lateral marketing*. We will illustrate it here, and we will describe the theory in the next chapter.

The new products and services described here were generated outside of the fixed category or market, and each one typically creates a new category or market. A product is taken and sufficiently transformed in order to make it appropriate for satisfying new needs or new persons/situations not considered previously.

The big advantage of this type of innovation is that instead of capturing a part of a market, it creates a new one.

Let's see some cases of innovations that redefined markets.

4.1 The Case of Cereal Bars

Cereals have many alimentary advantages: They are nourishing, rich in nutrients, and healthy. Hero, a company with various products in the food sector but a low market share in the breakfast cereal category, was thinking about how to gain market share in the cereals market.

The breakfast cereal category was highly fragmented and saturated with varieties.

Hero was not finding opportunities within this market. The solution was to redefine the utility of the cereals. Instead of marketing them as a breakfast complement, the thought occurred to sell them as a healthy snack at any time of the day.

But proposing that consumers carry cereals in bags and eat them with their hands is not a good solution. The idea occurred to adopt the shape of a different product that consumers were used to: chocolate bars. By merging the concepts of cereals and chocolate bars, a new category was born: cereal bars. A bit of caramel used as a "glue" enabled the small pieces of cereal to be delivered as a bar.

This product was a breakthrough and today we consider it something standard. Nevertheless, at the moment of the launch it was a real novelty and created a new consumption occasion.

Today Hero is one of the European leaders in the category of cereal bars, where Hero was the first to launch the product.

When we think about this, we ask ourselves: How is it possible to reach this idea? The innovation has not been made within the market "breakfast cereals for consumers." Hero did not seek a new positioning within the cereals category in the way it was normally perceived. Hero used the positive attributes of cereal but embedded them in another concept, a candy bar, and created a new convenience and a new category. This *lateral* marketing process expanded the market of cereals into new occasions.

4.2   The Case of Kinder Surprise

Kinder Surprise chocolate eggs are marketed as candies that are consumed by children and that contain toys for them to play with and collect. This product was launched in Italy in 1972.

Kinder Surprise grew very rapidly, conquering the hearts of all Europeans (from kids to adults). It was introduced in Canada in 1975. The product was an idea of and launched by Ferrero, an Italian entrepreneur.

When Kinder eggs were launched, the snacks market was structured mainly in the following subcategories: sweets, chewing gums, nuts, salty snacks, ice cream, and chocolates.

It was a fragmented market, and today it is even more fragmented.

Specifically, in the subcategory of chocolate bars, brand saturation was quite high. Chocolate bars of all sizes, varieties, and flavors competed to capture the attention and preferences not only of kids, but also of the parents. On many occasions parents purchase candies for their kids. Also, parents like to know and control what their children eat. This fact was very well captured by Ferrero.

When the firm decided to launch a new product in the subcategory of chocolate bars, it could have decided to introduce new flavors, ingredients, or designs to a chocolate bar concept (vertical innovation process).

Instead, Ferrero launched a novel concept: a chocolate egg with a toy inside—one of a long series of toys that kids can collect.

A toy inside a chocolate? If we were to consider an innovation within the chocolate bars market, it is not logical to think about a toy. We are candy manufacturers, aren't we?

Kinder Surprise eggs were advertised on TV and were positioned as a healthful product, rich in energy and carbohydrates. The size of the egg provides the appropriate portion of chocolate for consumption by a child. When the youngster opens the egg, he or she plays with the toy and does not ask for more chocolate. These two factors assured parents (the purchasers) that Kinder Surprise eggs are the right choice when selecting from among many candy options.

On the children's side, the concept has a triple attraction: they acquire chocolate, a toy, and a chance to collect toy spaceships, animals, monsters, and so on.

Kinder Surprise redefined the market of candies and chocolates by creating a new subcategory where it is the leader and no important competitor has yet appeared.

How many units would Ferrero have sold if it had launched a chocolate bar with peanuts, for example? Maybe it would have obtained 3 or 5 percent of market share.[1]

For some people it may be difficult to see the difference

---

[1] Instead, according to A. C. Nielsen's "Billion Dollar Brands" report for 2001, Kinder is the world's biggest chocolate brand, and the only one with sales of over $1 billion annually (*Advertising Age* estimates a 2000 global media spend of $667 million, of which $633 million was outside the United States, making it the world's #19 advertiser).

between a chocolate variety and a Kinder Surprise. Observe that Kinder Surprise adds the need of "playing" to the one of "eating." The market has been altered. A chocolate, if not changed, cannot satisfy a need of playing. Kinder Surprise does.

4.3   The Case of 7-Eleven Japan

The 7-Eleven convenience stores are found around the world. The 7-Eleven chain consists of outlets that sell all kinds of everyday foods, goods, and drinks 24 hours a day, without interruption. In Japan there are 7,000 outlets.

At the end of the 1990s, 7-Eleven Japan observed the growth of e-commerce and identified it as a possible threat to its business. Management had a brilliant idea. Instead of fighting against e-commerce, they decided to collaborate with it.

The stores became depot points for ordering, gathering, and paying for goods purchased on the Internet. Wherever you place the online order, you can pick it up and pay for it in 7-Eleven shops.

In this way, 7-Eleven is profiting from its excellent locations throughout Japan. And consumers can make their Internet purchases more cheaply, without having to pay for shipment to their houses. They collect their purchases at 7-Eleven stores at any time of the day or night.

How did 7-Eleven come up with this idea? The business of 7-Eleven is selling goods to end consumers, not the logistics business! If we start from a market definition based on the need to "buy food and other products in extended hours" we could hardly identify the opportunity to supply books or music CDs to Internet buyers. What market did 7-Eleven segment?

Again we have seen an innovation based on a strategy that falls outside of the natural market definition of a company's business.

4.4   The Case of Actimel, from Dannon

At the end of the 1990s, Dannon, one of the worldwide leaders of milk-based products, launched a new concept that created a radically new category in the milk sector: Actimel.

Ask any consumer who is aware of Actimel to say in which product category it belongs. This person will answer that Actimel is neither a yogurt nor a liquid such as a juice.

Actimel, this person would tell you, is a completely new product in itself. The concept is: a milk-based product that protects your organism from bacteria with ten thousand millions of L. casei immunitas.[2]

The interesting thing is that Actimel consumers are not people with stomach problems or other types of diseases. This product is not a prescription medicine. It is sold in the yogurts section of supermarkets to normal people who want to take care of themselves and who are concerned about eating healthily. The product is also addressed to children.

---

[2]Extracted from the voice-over of the Actimel TV commercial.

Millions of *L. casei immunitas* . . . what are they? Dannon, a trusted brand, says that these particles are defenses for your organism. If, additionally, Actimel has a good flavor (it really does) and is a milk-based product, consumers think it is good.

The package is small, and the quantity inside will not reduce your appetite. It is not a soft drink, a yogurt, or a juice, but millions of units have already been sold in Europe.

An original and breakthrough idea, don't you think? Only one or two other brands have launched similar concepts, and their share is under 10 percent. Would Dannon have obtained the same share with a new flavor of yogurt? And would sales have been as high? Actimel has hardly cannibalized the rest of Dannon's brands.

4.5   The Case of Food Stores inside Gas Stations

Gas stations have been, traditionally, places where cars are filled with fuel. That is their main purpose, but we have usually seen other products such as chewing gum, salty snacks, soft drinks, and sweets (impulse products, mainly) sold as well in gas stations.

Some years ago, gas stations started to carry newspapers and magazines, videos, even photo films. In some cases, the stores inside gas stations started to carry some food items.

In the past five years, gas stations' margins were threatened by constant increases in gasoline prices and taxes. The idea grew that the shops could be used as alternative ways of making money. Also, social changes (husband and wife active at jobs in a high percentage of households), together with short periods of time free for shopping, suggested that many customers going to the gas station to fill the car with gasoline would also buy more than impulse products, such as pasta, tomatoes, and so on.

Some gasoline distribution companies decided to open complete food stores at their gas stations. Now most cities have gas stations where you can buy fruit, bread, vegetables, water, coffee, sauces, and so on. Real food stores have been placed inside gas stations.

An important advantage of selling food at gas stations is that compared to what people pay for gasoline, the prices of the food may seem low enough. "Having to pay two dollars for a snack does not matter if I have spent $30 for gas." Consumers don't consider that the same snack costs one dollar in a normal supermarket.

Another advantage is that customers do not need to park their cars for shopping. They leave them beside the gas pumps or next to the store. They spend an average of five minutes inside the store buying products they ran out of at home.

The shops of gas stations are today generating an important percentage of the total earnings of these companies, since the margin of a gallon of gasoline is near 1 percent and the average margin of the store goods is above 50 percent!

Supermarkets inside gas stations! We have explained the logic of how this business started, but dedicate some seconds to think about it. Is it really logical that gas stations should become supermarkets?

4.6 The Case of the Cyber Café Concept

In cafés and cafeterias, it is customary to sell drinks, coffee, tea, food, sandwiches . . . but Internet access?

When the Internet was new and not available to everyone, someone thought about putting Internet access into a cafeteria setting to create the new type of business called a cyber café.

Cyber cafés are bars where you may or may not pay for what you drink, but do pay for how much time you are inside. At the table where the consumer will have a drink, a computer connected to the Internet is at his/her disposal. The customer can surf the Internet, send and receive e-mails, or chat online with others. Now it is not necessary to go for a drink with someone. You can go alone, order a coffee, and communicate with someone through the Internet!

Cyber cafés have become very popular and give to bar owners better margins per square foot than those obtained by charging for just a coffee or a soft drink.

Additionally, contrary to a normal bar, the more time customers remain, the better for the outlet. In a normal cafeteria, owners want customers to leave their tables soon so that new customers can sit down. In the case of the cyber café, this problem does not exist. The fees are related to time, so the profitability of the square foot is enormous.

Forget about the Internet for a while. What else could have been done with bars or cafeterias? Apply segmentation and positioning. We can think of a cafeteria for coffee gourmets or coffee lovers with more than 50 varieties of coffee.

We may think of a charming bar for couples or friends who want to hold a conversation. We may think of a fast cafeteria concept where you are served very quickly and a prepaid self-service system. Or we may think of a cafeteria for large groups, with tables for more than 10 people.

But: Internet? Observe that segmentation and positioning would not yield "cafeteria"+ "computers" if you think only of the cafeteria market.

4.7 The Case of "Be the Godfather of a Kid"

During many years, nonprofit organizations have raised money to alleviate global problems: third world hunger, AIDS, natural disasters, and so on.

Some donors had the feeling of not knowing how their money was used. "All right, I gave money for AIDS, but did it buy medicine or go into pay for the doctors?" People like to know.

Someone had the idea of helping donors see where their money is going. The campaign "Be the godfather of a kid" consists of a donation that goes directly to a specific youngster living in a specific city in a specific country. The fund-raising organization sends the donor a photograph of the child and his or her name.

A minimum donation allows this child to receive food and education from age 6 to 13.

This campaign has been one of the most successful in the history of fund-raising. The solution is to stop thinking about the total need of a country, but rather focus on the needs of a specific human being. The donee is tangible with a name and a face. This allows the donor to become involved with the fate of the donee.

Most other campaigns assure donors that their money is used to build homes or schools. But the resources needed are gathered from many people, so the assurance has a low impact on the satisfaction of the donor.

With the "Be the godfather of a kid" campaign, the donor's satisfaction is doubled. The donor not only sees the face of the child but also knows what the child is receiving.

4.8 The Case of "Big Brother" TV Contest

Previous to the launch of "Big Brother," a TV contest consisted of putting questions to contestants and giving prizes to the winners. There were participants and directors, a script, and a program lasting for one or two hours.

The "Big Brother" format radically changed the contest concept: no script, no specific competitions, no interruptions. The contest consists of introducing 12 people inside a house, completely isolated from the exterior, recorded without interruption. The TV audience observes their lives, behavior, and personalities and votes for the preferred ones. Every week (as in the mystery novel by Agatha Christie, *Ten Little Indians*), one is eliminated and expelled from the house.

"Big Brother" has been a leader in audience buildup in many countries. It is the reality show taken to the extreme (like in the film *The Truman Show*, but with the participants' permission).

Would a new quiz show have obtained the same success? Probably not.

"Big Brother" represents a change in the paradigm to "TV contest + real life."

4.9   The Case of Huggies Pull-Ups

It is known that, between two and three years old, children are initiated in the difficult task of phasing out diapers. It is a stage in which children must learn to tell that they have to satisfy a need, so they will not spot their clothes. Many children pass through this stage with difficulties and frustration.

From the manufacturers' perspective, diapers as a mass market product have a target market that hardly goes beyond three-year-olds. The intelligent question is: How can I continue selling the diaper beyond the age when the need for it ends?

The brilliant idea, in this case, was to transform a diaper into something similar to panties for children. With Pull-Ups training pants toddlers don't have the feeling that we are putting them in a baby diaper, and we make them feel better, older, and more like an adult. At the same time, if the child cannot stop the impulse, a picture disappears in the exterior of the training pants, signaling that something has happened.

This avoids frustrating the boy/girl, but rather teaches while substituting Pull-Ups for grown-up underclothes.

Notice that with appropriate changes, diaper companies have managed to extend sales to older children. One could never achieve this using only ideas stemming from the current diaper market. We are not proposing to think about how to sell a product to the person who does not need it, but rather how to modify it so that the person *will* need it.

Not all lateral marketing examples correspond to recent innovations. The two examples that follow were created some time ago, but were also originated using lateral marketing thinking.

4.10   The Case of Barbie

"It was the late 1950s when Ruth Handler noticed her daughter playing with paper dolls and imagining them in grown-up roles. Since most dolls at the time were baby dolls, Ruth envisioned one that would inspire little girls to think about what they wanted to be when they grew up. Ruth created a teenage fashion model doll named Barbie (after her daughter), and the rest is history."[3]

Up to then, dolls varied in price, size, nationality, design, dress, complements, accessories, color of eyes, and color of hair, but few thought of a doll that was not a baby. Why? A doll *is* a baby. This belief leads to modifications in any attributes of a baby in order to create new dolls.

It is not surprising that the idea came to a person who did not work in a doll company. Such people probably would have been blind to the possibility of an adult-looking doll.

---

[3]Text extracted from the web site of Mattel.

"Barbie, the world's best selling doll, has been an integral part of the lives of millions of young girls. Her timeless appeal has resulted in a dedicated legion of fans that love to collect her. From celebrities like Cher to the glamorous fashion designer theme, the fabulous Barbie Collectibles line includes more than 600 dolls."[4]

Barbie is the result of thinking about dolls in a different way. The source of this type of thinking will be analyzed in detail in the next chapter.

4.11   The Case of Walkman

Walkman originated from a coincidence. In 1978, Sony engineers tried to design a small portable tape recorder with stereo sound, but the recording sound quality was not good enough.

One day Masaru Ibuka,[5] honorary president of Sony, suggested combining lightweight head phones (which were under development in another division) with the tape recorder because although it had a low quality of recording, it had a good quality when reproducing sound. Ibuka asked to eliminate every function except playing. This was not a logical idea, since at that time an audiotape that could not record was difficult to market.

The new product was launched with a small advertising budget of $100,000. Despite the small budget, the idea and

---

[4]Text extracted from the web site of Mattel.
[5]See Michael Michalko, *Thinkertoys: A Handbook of Business Creativity for the 90s* (Berkeley, CA: Ten Speed Press, 1991).

product were so good that Walkman became one of the most successful marketing innovations in history. It made Sony a leader and generated strong cash flow for many other projects.

If Sony had limited its thinking to hi-fi, it would have come up with just another tape recorder for home usage. If it had used the marketing process of segmentation and positioning, stemming from the market definition and persons/situations of tape recorders in 1978, it might have developed new products such as:

- Hi-fi for music lovers, with sophisticated functions.
- Hi-fi with modern design, for those with an innovative lifestyle.
- High-power hi-fi for the youngest.
- Low-priced hi-fi for low to medium social classes.

To think about Walkman, the company had to add to audio equipment the concept of mobility. Someone had to think of a portable product on the person. Walkman originated the category today called "personal audio," which moves millions of dollars all over the world and where Sony is leader.

Summary

We have described examples of innovations that at the time were hugely successful and which restructured markets.

There are many more. In fact, any new category that opens up could be an example. Al Ries and Jack Trout recommend the strategy of opening categories when there are too many competitors.[6]

New market or category creation is the most efficient way to compete in mature markets where microsegmentation and an excess of brands do not leave room for new opportunities.

We are living in times when different types of industries are converging and creating new categories. We talk about "eductainment." We talk about the car as an office. We are combining TV with the Internet. Pharmaceuticals (which came from chemistry) are increasingly coming from biotechnology.

These types of businesses can also emerge as a consequence of a lateral marketing process, whose need will be examined in the next chapter.

---

[6]See Al Ries and Jack Trout, *The 22 Immutable Laws of Marketing: Violate Them at Your Own Risk.* (New York: HarperBusiness, 1993).

The Need for Lateral Marketing to Complement Vertical Marketing

The two previous chapters describe two radically different ways of innovating: the one that consists of modulations within a given market (Chapter 3) and the one that restructures markets by creating a new category through new uses, situations, or targets with the appropriate changes in our product (Chapter 4). Figure 5.1 describes these two processes.

We have named the first one *vertical marketing*. It works inside a market definition, applying segmentation and positioning, modulating the current product or service in order to create varieties. It goes from the global toward the concrete through a sequential and logical thinking process, a vertical thinking process.

We have named the second one *lateral marketing*. It restructures the existing information and goes from the concrete to the global through less selective thinking, but rather more exploratory, probabilistic, provocative, and creative thinking.

Someone might think that we will argue that lateral marketing is superior to vertical marketing. Absolutely not. Both are necessary and complementary. Moreover, lateral market-

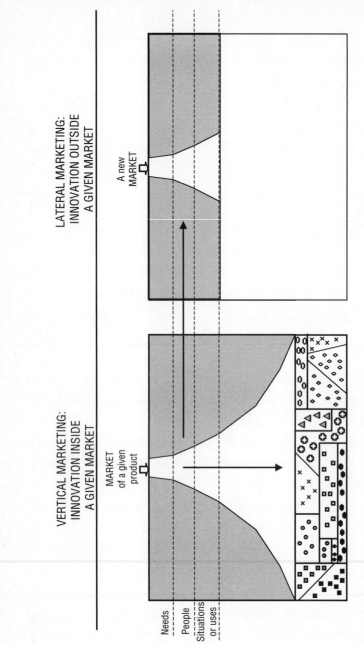

VERTICAL MARKETING:
INNOVATION INSIDE
A GIVEN MARKET

LATERAL MARKETING:
INNOVATION OUTSIDE
A GIVEN MARKET

MARKET
of a given
product

A new
MARKET

Needs
People
Situations
or uses

Figure 5.1 Vertical versus Lateral Marketing

ing cannot be developed fully without vertical marketing since the latter will produce more variations after a new category is discovered.

Lateral marketing is a complement of vertical marketing.

Here we will compare both types of processes with regard to the following aspects:

- What they are based on.
- How they work.
- What they allow.
- Their sources of volume.
- When they are more appropriate.
- Whose responsibility each of them is.

We will show how the two processes are complementary and how each provides what the other lacks. This means that successful companies will use both processes in their search for innovations.

5.1   Basis of Vertical versus Lateral Marketing

The vertical marketing process obliges us to first define the market. Vertical marketing uses the definition of the market to create competitive advantages. The innovation is done inside this definition. The market definition allows consistency with our mission when launching an innovation to expand our business.

Lateral marketing is based on seeking an expansion by approaching one or more needs, uses, targets, or situations that we discarded in the market definition of the product or service. But this means that our product needs to be altered. In Chapter 4, we showed how several products were altered by applying lateral marketing thinking:

- Kinder Surprise *adds the use* of playing to a chocolate.
- 7-Eleven *adds the use* of point of delivery to its shops.
- Cereal bars *add the situation* of snacking to cereals, which were conceived only for the breakfast occasion.
- Actimel *adds the need* of protecting from bacteria to a yogurt.
- Gas station stores *add the use* of food goods purchase to gas stations.
- Cyber cafés *add the use* of the Internet to a café.
- "Be the godfather of a kid" *adds the need* of adoption to a donation.
- "Big Brother" *adds the target* teenager to the followers of TV contests.
- Huggies Pull-Ups *adds the target*: kids who don't need diapers.
- Barbie *adds the need* of being a teenager to the use of dolls.
- Walkman *adds the use* of an audio player in occasions that would have been impossible with the existing solutions.

So, lateral marketing implies that we will have to make an important transformation in our product. The output of the process is not under the same control as in vertical thinking. We may come out with an idea that implies redefining our market, our channels, even the mission of our company. Lateral marketing will explore all the areas where the vertical marketing process doesn't take us.

Figure 5.2 shows clearly the areas examined by each type of thinking.

Lateral marketing works in the areas where vertical marketing does not. Lateral marketing restructures a product by adding needs, uses, situations, or targets unreachable without the appropriate changes.

5.2 How Lateral Marketing Works versus Vertical Marketing

Vertical marketing is based on logical and sequential thinking. The famous author Edward de Bono introduced the concept of lateral thinking and defined it as "a set of processes destined to the use of information in such a way that generates creative ideas through a perspicacious restructuring of concepts stored in the mind."[1]

---

[1]See Edward de Bono, *Lateral Thinking: A Textbook of Creativity* (London: Pelican Books, 1970), Preface.

79

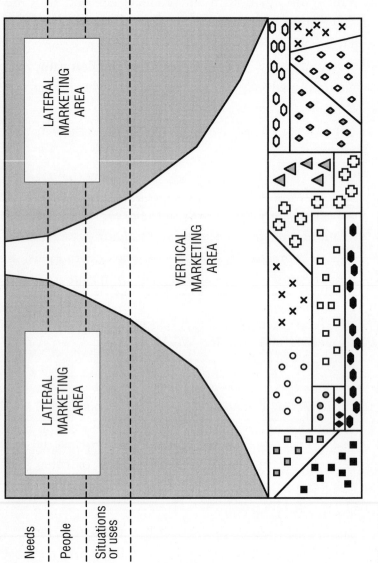

Figure 5.2   Areas Examined by Lateral versus Vertical Thinking

Lateral thinking could be summarized in two parts:

1. The analysis of the models (the fixed concepts we have in mind).
2. The techniques for altering these models (ways to transform them).

The lateral marketing process creates, whereas the vertical marketing process selects.

Following Edward de Bono, there have been other authors who have developed more techniques for restructuring than the ones identified by de Bono.

The list that follows reproduces the differences between lateral and vertical thinking included in Chapter 2 of Edward de Bono's book *Lateral Thinking*, but applied to marketing:

- The lateral marketing process opens up new directions whereas vertical marketing moves along a specified direction.
- Lateral marketing is provocative, whereas vertical marketing is analytical.
- Vertical marketing follows a sequence, whereas lateral marketing can jump into other products or categories without apparent sense in order to capture possible ideas and provoke changes.
- Vertical marketing has to be correct in all its steps. Lateral marketing does not need to be correct. If the final result is valid, the process is also considered valid.

- Vertical marketing selects by discarding. Lateral marketing does not discard any alternative that might lead to a new concept.

- Lateral marketing can use categories or products not related to our product whereas vertical marketing excludes concepts outside of our potential market definition.

- Lateral marketing follows the less evident ways, whereas vertical marketing proceeds in a sequential and evident way.

- Lateral marketing is a probabilistic process, whereas vertical marketing is a finite process.

Lateral thinking consists of analyzing models and provoking changes in the models. Vertical marketing uses a logical process. Lateral marketing uses a probabilistic process.

5.3 Effects That Lateral Marketing Provokes in the Markets versus Vertical Marketing

In Chapters 2 and 3 we described what vertical marketing can do. To summarize:

- It produces ideas for *enlarging the size of a given market*.
- It helps *convert potential customers into current customers* in a given market.

- It allows being present in *all possible situations* where our product can be within its current market.
- It helps *increase penetration* toward the maximum level in the given market.
- It allows finding new positioning axes within the product/service market.

Nevertheless, in mature markets and in the long term, innovations generated by vertical marketing produce low incremental volume, and considerable cannibalization occurs.

The innovations that come from lateral marketing, in contrast, create new categories or subcategories resulting from one or several effects:

1. *A lateral product can restructure markets by creating new categories or subcategories.* For example, the launch of Walkman by Sony radically restructured the market of electronic goods, since it converted millions of young potential consumers (no market at that moment) into current consumers of personal audio products.
2. *It can reduce the volume of other products within the given market.* For example, Kinder Surprise has reduced the sales of not only chocolates and other candies, but also nuts and other salty snacks. Barbie has taken a huge percentage of sales of baby type dolls.
3. *The lateral product can sometimes generate volume without hurting other volume.* Most of the volume of Actimel, for example, is incremental, since it is not a substitute for yogurt and its consumption takes place in the

morning, before leaving home for work or school, as a breakfast complement. Actimel generates volume by itself, not by stealing from other categories.

4. *If sales are not incremental, the lateral product will take volume from several categories.* For example, cereal bars are consumed as a snack and are affecting the volume of several categories, such as chocolates, salty snacks, and even yogurts consumed as a healthy snack. This seriously damages other categories (see Figure 5.3).

In this sense, the main advantage of lateral marketing is that it overcomes the problem of fragmentation, which is one of the main sources of the difficulties for succeeding with new products.

5.4 Source of Volume

Innovations coming from *vertical marketing* obtain volume from two sources:

1. In early stages of the life cycle, volume comes from incumbent players together with a number of potential buyers who have been attracted by the innovation.
2. In later stages of the product life cycle, incremental volume is lower and comes from product competitors' market share losses.

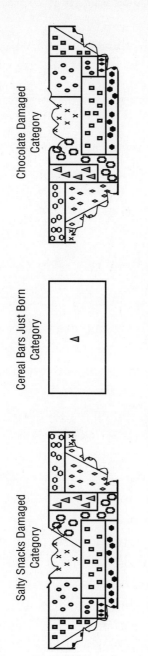

Salty Snacks Damaged
Category

Cereal Bars Just Born
Category

Chocolate Damaged
Category

Figure 5.3 Lateral Product Taking Volume from Other Categories

85

The volume of a new product arising from *lateral marketing* comes from two sources:

1. Volume comes from generic competitors, affecting several categories.

2. Sometimes there is no other referent. When there is not a clear substitute and the innovation has activated an underlying need, volume comes from the product itself. This is less frequent, however.

5.5 Situations Where Each Type of Marketing Is More Appropriate

Both marketing processes are important. Table 5.1 shows the situations when one might be more appropriate than the other. In this sense, certain aspects or considerations need to be taken into account:

Innovations that come from a vertical marketing process are easier for customers to assimilate and understand.

Consumers and customers need to understand quickly the utility of new products that appear in the markets for the first time. If this comprehension is not immediate, the chance of succeeding strongly decreases.

A *vertical marketing* innovation is much easier for consumers to assimilate and adopt. Since it occurs within an existing category, its comprehension is almost immediate. Less effort needs to be spent on consumer education, and trying the product comes about earlier.

In contrast, *lateral marketing* innovations, if they are very

Table 5.1 Appropriate Situations for Vertical versus Lateral Marketing

Vertical Marketing	Lateral Marketing
More adequate in markets of recent creation that are in a first stage of development	More adequate for mature markets where growth is zero
For developing markets and for making them larger through varieties and through the conversion of potential customers into current customers	For creating markets or categories from scratch, for merging different types of businesses, for reaching targets we could never reach with our current product, and for finding new uses
Under a less risky business philosophy	Under a more risky business philosophy
When few resources are available	When there are more resources available or business is ready to invest and wait
When a secure, even low, incremental volume needs to be ensured	When we want to reach a high volume of business
In order to defend markets, by fragmenting them through the number of brands and, therefore, making markets less attractive for new entrants	To attack markets with a generic competition from outside the arena of direct competitors
To innovate stemming from our mission and keeping our business focus	To redefine our mission, and to seek other markets

different, will need more time for their assimilation. This happened when consumers were slow to patronize cyber cafés or purchase Barbie dolls.

Lateral marketers must work more slowly in disseminating the innovation to pioneers, early adopters, initial majority adopters, and late majority adopters. Efforts for education, communication, and sales of a lateral marketing innovation are higher.

Many companies, in choosing between two versions of a new product to offer, will opt for the easier one, even though the other may be really new and different. The expected profit is calculated by multiplying the probability of success by the expected total margin:

ROI = Success probability × Volume

Expected profit = Success probability × Volume × Margin

Vertical marketing innovations have a high probability of success, but a low incremental volume in mature and fragmented markets. Normally, this gives poor results.

Lateral marketing innovations, on the contrary, may have a much lower probability of success, but if they do succeed, the obtained volume can be extremely high.

Compare the results that Sony would have obtained if, instead of the Walkman, it had launched another version of audio equipment for the household. Compare the results of launching Barbie versus a new blond baby doll that laughs and says "Mama."

Innovations that come from a vertical marketing process are easier to create.

Doing variations of existing products or services is something that we are used to. Vertical thinking is logical and sequential. Variations and modulations that stem from a prefixed scheme require less creative effort than trying to modify schemes or models.

In contrast, we have not been trained in lateral thinking or out-of-the-box thinking. We have not learned it in school and its exercise is basic for its application.

Furthermore, there are few marketing techniques available for doing it. There are many books about innovation and creativity, but these techniques are seldom linked to the marketing process or to marketing theories. Not having a marketing framework for thinking laterally inhibits doing lateral marketing. Creativity is a result and not a process. For doing lateral marketing, professionals need a process.

Part of this book's objective is to develop a framework and have marketing professionals share tools and techniques for lateral marketing.

Vertical marketing innovations are faster and cheaper to manufacture.

Normally, a *vertical marketing* innovation can be made more easily, more cheaply, and faster. The short life cycle of products requires frenetic activity in new product development. This results in vertical marketing innovations occurring more frequently in companies: "The urgent does not leave time for the important."

In perfumery, for example, the company only has to develop another fragrance, produce a new bottle, print different labels and boxes, and presto! A new brand. Perfume companies are in a war of new brands. Each Christmas there appear in Spain nearly 100 new perfume brands.

In contrast, *lateral marketing* innovations may require important investments in production systems. Sometimes they even require the implementation of a new business. For example, Kinder Surprise manufacturing is much more complex than just producing a chocolate bar.

Lateral marketing innovations are more difficult to produce and more difficult for consumers or customers to assimilate, but the ROI can be much higher, because volume can be incremental or come from generic competitors affecting several categories.

5.6 Responsibility of Creating in the Markets

Vertical marketing uses the left part of our brain (the logical). *Lateral marketing* calls for using the right part of our brain (the creative, the intuitive). The application of both at the same time will offer powerful marketing capacities.

Creativity is not a task that a company can assign to anyone. Some of it depends on encouraging unique individuals to come up with brilliant ideas. "The visionary, the creative will do it."

Yet even creativity may lie in a method. Wolfgang Amadeus Mozart, Leonardo da Vinci, and Thomas Edison had methods for creating. It is our objective in the next chapter to develop a lateral marketing creative process.

Advertising campaigns are delegated to the creative directors of advertising agencies; new product concepts are delegated to marketing researchers; new product ideas are expected from the research and development (R&D) department.

Today, the opportunities for creating new categories have to rely on creativity, on using the right part of the brain. And this should be an additional function of the marketing departments, one that it must embrace wholeheartedly.

Lateral marketing will allow marketers to perform creative functions without relying on an accidental idea. Defining a process is necessary. Lateral marketing will help to use the right part of the brain within a marketing framework.

Summary

Lateral marketing does not replace *vertical marketing*. It is a complement (see Table 5.2). It is possible to use the discarded needs, targets, uses, situations, and attributes in order to think up fresh new product ideas.

The aim is to consider our market as a nonfixed model and work on it with the objective of restructuring it for obtaining a new market. It is hoped that the lateral marketing process will generate new categories, redefine businesses, and expand missions of companies.

The next chapter will introduce and propose a whole process that will allow marketing professionals to apply lateral marketing and in the process produce bright new ideas.

Table 5.2   Comparison of Vertical and Lateral Marketing

	Vertical Marketing	*Lateral Marketing*
It is based on . . .	The set of needs, persons, and situations or uses of our product	The discarded needs, persons, situations, or uses of our product
	Our mission, innovating from what we want to be as a company	Being open to redefine our mission if necessary, but innovating from our current offer
It works . . .	Vertically, following the marketing process	Laterally, out of the marketing process
In an early stage it allows . . .	Development of markets and conversion of potential customers into current customers	Creation of markets, categories, or subcategories, and capability of reaching targets/situations nonreachable with the existing products
In a later stage it allows . . .	Low incrementality, but it is an easy-to-sell novelty	High incrementality, but it is a more risky option
Its source of volume is . . .	Market share of product competitors, and the conversion of potential customers and situations into current ones	Totally incremental, without affecting other markets, or by taking from many other categories market share of generic competition

Table 5.2 *(Continued)*

	Vertical Marketing	Lateral Marketing
It is appropriate when . . .	Early stage of the life cycle of a market or product (growing phase)	Mature stage of the life cycle of a market or product
	Low-risk strategies Low resources available	High-risk strategies High resources available
	For defending markets by fragmenting them	For attacking markets from outside them (with substitutes)
It is current responsibility of . . .	Marketing departments	Not always marketing departments, but of: • Creative agencies • Entrepreneurs • Small and medium companies • Engineers, R&D departments

Defining the Lateral Marketing Process

6.1 Lateral Marketing Definition

Lateral marketing is a work process which, when applied to existing products or services, produces innovative new products and services that cover needs, uses, situations, or targets not currently covered and, therefore, is a process that offers a high chance of creating new categories or markets.

So, it is important to keep in mind that:

- Lateral marketing is a *process*.
- This process is *methodical*; it follows an organized sequence.
- It is applied to an existing *object* (a product, a service, or a business).
- It produces an *innovation* that in many cases may be a new subcategory, category, or market.

6.1.1 Objectives of Lateral Marketing

Lateral marketing can provide an answer to any of these questions:

- What other needs can I satisfy with my product if I change it?
- What other needs can I incorporate in my product to make it different?
- What nonpotential consumers could I reach by changing my product?
- What other things can I offer to my current consumers/clients?
- In what other situations can my product be used if I change it?
- What other products can cover the situations or uses of my current product?
- What else can my product be used for?
- What other products can be generated stemming from my current product?
- What substitutes can I generate in order to attack a given product?

Let's now explore how to make this possible.

6.2 Logic of Creativity

Creative thinking follows three simple steps:[1]

---

[1]Edward de Bono analyzed in a detailed way the steps necessary for thinking creatively. See *Serious Creativity: Using the Power of Lateral Thinking to Create New Ideas* (New York: HarperBusiness, 1992).

1. Select a *focus*.

2. Make a *lateral displacement* for generating a stimulus.

3. Make a *connection*.

A *focus* may be anything that we want to concentrate on. A focus can be a problem to solve, an objective to achieve, or just a simple object. For example, "flower" can be a possible focus (see Figure 6.1).

A *lateral displacement* is an interruption in the middle of a logical thought sequence. For example, one possible lateral movement of the fact that "flowers die" could be "flowers that never die" (see Figure 6.2).

Figure 6.1   Focus

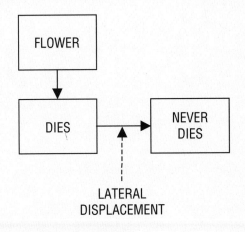

Figure 6.2   Lateral Displacement

99

Such an idea may or may not make sense, but it is provocative.[2]

There are concrete and specific techniques for creating lateral movements such as this one. We will show techniques later.

A lateral displacement applied to a focus normally creates a disconnection, a gap. Note in Figure 6.3 that there is a gap between "flower" and "never dies." This gap, which appears as a problem, is in fact the source of creativity. The gap is our *stimulus*. Why?

Because our brain is a self-organized system that forces connections continually. If two unconnected ideas are exposed to our mind, our thinking will make the necessary additional *movements* until a logical *connection* is made.

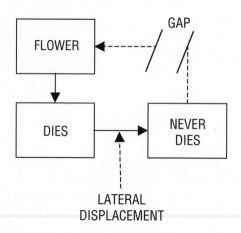

Figure 6.3   Gap Created by Lateral Displacement

---

[2]The lateral displacement is equivalent to the concept "provocation" normally used in creativity.

For example, we need to move the concept "flower" some-where until it is consistent with the idea that it never dies. We will have to modify something; otherwise these elements will never be connected.

One way is to ask ourselves: Under what situations will a flower never die? If a flower is made of cloth or plastic, then it would never die. We have found a new concept: "artificial flower." The connection has been made, and the gap has been solved (see Figure 6.4).

This is exactly the origin of creativity. **Innovations are a result of connecting two ideas which, in principle, had no apparent or immediate connection.**

Summarizing:

- "Flower" is the *focus*.
- "Never dies" is a *displacement* of a flower characteristic.
- The gap between "flower" and "never dies" is a *stimulus*.

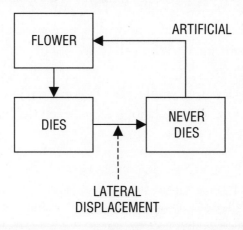

Figure 6.4   Connection

- The *movement* is changing the material of the flower.

- The *connection* is a new idea or concept: an "artificial flower."

The tricky thing here is that, a posteriori, any idea or solution to be valid has to be explained logically. But would we have found that solution without the stimulus? Normally, no. The lateral displacement techniques put in front of us stimuli that logical thinking would never generate. This is the reason why stimuli are necessary for innovating.

6.3   Similarities between Humor and Creative Thinking

The logic of creativity is very similar to humor.[3] A funny story consists of someone describing an initial situation (*focus*) and a *displacement* in order to generate a *gap* (change of perspective at the middle of the funny story). The listeners have to search for logic and will make a *movement* in order to *connect* both ideas. When they are connected this will provoke laughter.

Take as an example the famous remark of Groucho Marx: "I don't care to belong to any club that will accept me as a member."

---

[3]Edward de Bono usually uses the analogy between humor and creativity to facilitate an easier understanding of how creative thinking works. See *Serious Creativity: Using the Power of Lateral Thinking to Create New Ideas* (New York: HarperBusiness, 1992).

The first part of the sentence is the *focus* (we think that he is going to specify a certain type of club composed of people he does not like). The lateral *displacement* is to talk of himself being accepted by the club in the next phrase. The *gap* is that Groucho would never accept membership in any club that would accept him. The sentence has no sense at all. There is no way to solve it, unless we force a movement. The *movement* is to seek another perspective of the whole sentence in order for it to be logical. It makes sense only if the meaning is another: Groucho is telling us that he recognizes that his personality is unacceptable to anyone, even to himself. Then we laugh. This thinking process happens in less than a second.

6.4   Importance of Understanding the Logic of Creativity

When someone discovers and integrates how creativity works, then its mystery disappears. Creativity is not a magical capacity; it is the result of these three steps, which can be followed by anyone.

If someone wants to apply lateral marketing, it is essential to fully understand each step. One needs to know which step he or she is working on and be completely aware of what he or she is intending.

If, for example, I am thinking about the focus, I must be aware that I am only preparing myself for generating a displacement. If I am thinking about a possible displacement, I have to be aware that I am just generating a stimulus for later use. Or if I am thinking about a movement for making a connection, I have to be aware that I am working on changing my stimulus in order to make it logical.

The logic of creativity consists of taking an element, displacing laterally one aspect of it, and connecting the gap that has been provoked. The logic of creativity follows a process similar to that of humor.

6.5   The Three Steps of Lateral Marketing

After a product or service is chosen, the steps of a lateral marketing process are:

Step 1: Choose a focus where we want to generate a lateral displacement.

Step 2: Provoke a lateral displacement for generating a gap.

Step 3: Think about ways to connect the gap.

6.5.1   Choosing a Product or Service

Lateral marketing starts with a product or a service. We have two choices:

1. Choosing the product or service we market.
2. Choosing a product or service where we have difficulties competing.

It may seem surprising that a marketing process starts by selecting a product, when the marketing mantra is to think on people and not on products. The reason is that creativity stems from concrete things. This fact has been observed by many geniuses: Edison said that an innovation was just another way of observing the same reality. The Albert Einstein's relativity theory was a result of observing the same effects of someone walking inside a train from two different perspectives.

Creative thinking works from the bottom up, from the concrete to the general. It is inductive, not deductive.

The lateral marketing process begins with choosing a product or service.

6.5.2   Step 1: Choosing a Focus in the Marketing Process

Once a product has been chosen, how can we select a focus within it? Is a focus any aspect of the product?

One of the best ways of innovating is by splitting into parts something that is an accepted model. We have to take into account that a model is a given combination of pieces. You can change it only if you split it into pieces.

Thus, the best way to break a product or service into pieces for marketing purposes is to use the scheme of vertical marketing. There is no better way.

Why? For several reasons. First, the vertical marketing process is a scheme that all marketing professionals use, and this facilitates people working together. If everyone has their own particular way of dissecting, then it is difficult to work as a team.

The second reason is that the vertical marketing scheme is complete. It contains everything that is relevant from a commercial point of view: the need, the use, the brand, the price.

The third reason is that it has been used so much that it is convenient.

Nevertheless, the vertical marketing scheme has many components. Just within promotion policies, we can think of more than 10 aspects that can become a possible focus (e.g., the message, the advertising media, the style of the communication, the target of the campaign, the unique selling proposition).

So, we need to simplify.

Our proposition is that all the pieces of the vertical marketing process should be grouped into three main levels for lateral marketing purposes, as shown in Figure 6.5:

1. The *market definition* level.
2. The *product* level.
3. The *rest of the marketing mix* level.

If we apply lateral marketing techniques to our market definition, we say that we are doing lateral marketing with focus on the market (see Figure 6.6). For example, let's take the diapers market. Trying to modify the market of diapers (e.g., diapers for children who start to abandon them) would be lateral marketing with focus on market.

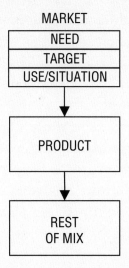

Figure 6.5   Three Levels of Lateral Marketing

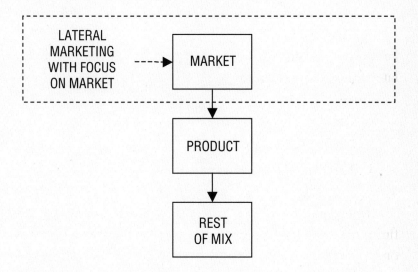

Figure 6.6   Focus on Market

If we apply the techniques to our product definition, we say that we are doing lateral marketing with focus on product (see Figure 6.7). Trying to modify a diaper, with no other objective than finding an innovation, would be lateral marketing with focus on product.

And, finally, if we are using the rest of the marketing mix as an input for lateral marketing techniques, we say that we are doing lateral marketing with focus on mix (see Figure 6.8). So, trying to modify the marketing mix of diapers (e.g., diapers being bought on a payment plan) would be lateral marketing with focus on the mix.

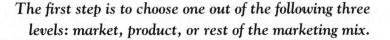

The first step is to choose one out of the following three levels: market, product, or rest of the marketing mix.

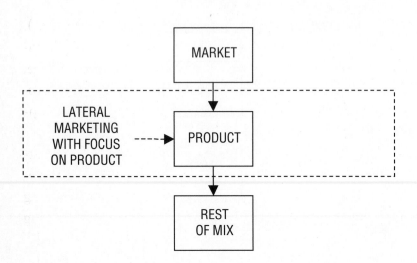

Figure 6.7 Focus on Product

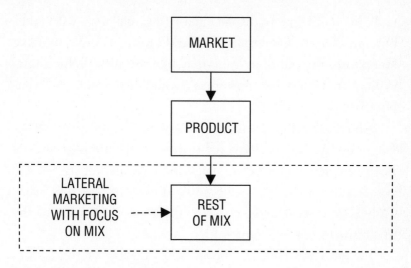

Figure 6.8   Focus on Mix

But, why have we split the vertical marketing process in these three groups and not others?

The product level includes the tangible solution (what). The market includes the utility or need (why), the consumer/buyer (who), and the uses or situations (when, where, with whom). The marketing mix, in contrast, does not question who, why, when, or what is being marketed. It just contains *how* it will be sold.

The lateral marketing process continues by displacing laterally *only one* of these elements. Thus, the proposed three-level distinction is absolutely crucial, because creating disconnections (lateral displacements) consists of creating gaps by moving something while letting something be fixed.

Let's observe what happens in each of the three cases.

For example, if we choose the *product level* as the focus

and make any type of displacement (e.g., cafeteria with computers), then we need to find a market for it, in order to make an opportunity out of it. Who may like this idea? Which is its utility? In which circumstances would "cafeteria" + "computer" be accepted?

The marketing mix is not under consideration yet. Why? Because if we have discovered utility in the stimulus, it does not make sense (yet) to consider *how* to market it. So, the connection of the gap needs to be done with the first level. Only then does it make sense to think about the rest of the marketing mix (see Figure 6.9).

Imagine now that we choose as a focus the *market level* of (say) motorbikes. We select within the market level elements the situation of being used on the ground. We apply any lateral displacement technique and propose that the motorbike has to run on water. Today such a product is familiar to us, but

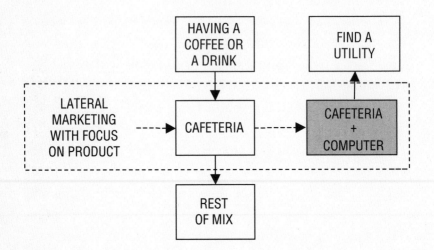

Figure 6.9 Focus on Product: Combining Cafeterias with the Internet

imagine it is not. The proposition would sound absurd. It should have no wheels, and the motor should be at the rear, like in a boat. (See Figure 6.10.)

Again, the mix was not under consideration because we do not have a physical solution for the new utility (motorbikes on water). It makes no sense to dedicate time (yet) to think of how to sell it.

Finally, imagine that we choose the *marketing mix* level and apply it to (say) cellular phones. We apply a lateral displacement of the price, saying that the user is always paying, even when the mobile mobile is disconnected.

Observe that levels one and two have not been touched yet—so they remain connected! So, the inconsistency has to be solved at the same level where it happened. (See Figure 6.11.)

We still have a product and a utility that make sense (the

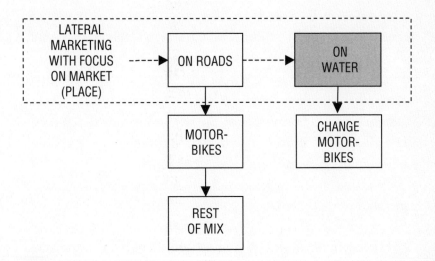

Figure 6.10   Focus on Market: Changing Situation of Motorbikes

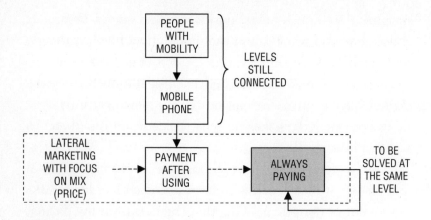

Figure 6.11 Focus on Marketing Mix Applied to Cellular Phones

cellular phone for making calls in mobility situations). The only thing we have done is provoke a gap within the *how*, but the *what* and *why* remain unaltered.

A possible way to solve this gap is by establishing a fixed tariff per month for each user, based on his first-year average consumption. Each month the customer receives an e-mail where he can see if he is over or under his level of expenditure, so he can be more cautious the next month or talk more if he has accumulated credit. Every six months, the extra consumption would be charged or the remaining money returned. The customer controls expenditure and the operator ensures a minimum usage of the phone each month.

See that we have generated a new subproduct, a subcategory, but not a fully new product or utility.

Important implications should be considered when choosing the focus at any of the three levels.

Working with or without an Objective   Generating a displacement in the first level keeps our product fixed, so the gap is that we will place it into other settings (e.g., beer for motorcycle riders, orange juice at night, apples at a hotel reception desk, food sold at gas stations, milk after playing tennis).

Choosing the market as a focus implies working with a clear objective. We know the market we want to reach. We have to think of a physical solution. We propose an impossible utility, target, use, or situation and seek a solution that is valid in the new context. So, lateral marketing with focus on the level of market is lateral marketing with an objective definition.

By choosing either of the two other levels, in contrast, especially the product level, we are just displacing the product, and then we observe what we obtain in order to find out what it can be used for. It is more heuristic, more exploratory, and more probabilistic.

We propose a new product and try to adjust it in order to find a valid context for it (utility, target, use, and situation).

Lateral marketing with focus on product (or on the mix) is lateral marketing without an objective (apart from the one of creating an innovation).

The Focus   The focus determines the level of the vertical marketing sequence where the first displacement will occur. The higher the focus in the vertical marketing sequence, the higher the chance to create a new category.

The Anchors   After choosing the level, we still have to select which specific marketing aspect will be our focus.

If we select as a focus the product level of computers, are

we going to displace the keyboard? screen? the processor? These are the anchors that make up our product.

These three could be interesting elements to displace. If we move any of these anchors, we will be escaping from our current product. But if we select the mouse of the computer as our focus, it will be difficult to generate a breakthrough innovation, because the mouse is not an essential element of a computer.

We will go into this with more detail in Chapters 7 and 8, where the treatment of anchors will be developed.

Focusing on the market level or the product level for making a displacement generates a gap between these two elements. This will easily lead toward the creation of new categories. Focusing on the rest of the mix leaves the product and the market connected. Displacements will lead toward subcategories or innovative commercial formulas.

6.5.3 Step 2: Generating a Marketing Gap

The basis of lateral marketing is creating a gap. If there is no gap, there is no lateral marketing. The absence of a gap after a displacement has taken place indicates that we are doing vertical marketing instead of lateral marketing.

A gap exists only if it requires us to jump. The only way of generating a gap is by interrupting logical thinking temporarily.

How can we interrupt our logical thinking if we have been trained all our life to think logically? Edward de Bono, in his book *Lateral Thinking*, introduced specific techniques. Since then, many authors have proposed many ways for creating displacements for interrupting logical thinking.

But almost all the techniques are based on six basic operations.[4] When we use them, we are conscious that we are not using logical thinking. The operations are:

- Substitute it.
- Invert it.
- Combine it.

---

[4]Alex Osborn, a pioneer creativity professor, suggested seven questions that stimulate ideas. Bob Eberle named them "SCAMPER." Each letter of the word SCAMPER represents one of seven questions: Substitute?, Combine?, Adapt?, Modify?, Put?, Eliminate or reduce?, Reorder or invert? We have analyzed more than 250 creativity techniques of creativity manuals and creative business books: *Cracking Creativity: The Secrets of Creative Genius* by Michael Michalko, *Thinkertoys: A Handbook of Business Creativity* by Michael Michalko, *Lateral Thinking* by Edward de Bono, *Serious Creativity* by Edward de Bono, *Why Didn't I Think of That?* by Charles McCoy, *A Whack on the Side of the Head* by Roger van Oech, *The New Drawing on the Right Part of the Brain* by Betty Edwards, *101 Creative Problem Solving Techniques* by James M. Higgins, and *Creative Problem Solver's Toolbox* by Richard Fobes. This analysis has told us that almost any creative technique essentially relies on one or more of the six lateral displacement techniques proposed in this book.

- Exaggerate it.
- Eliminate it.
- Reorder it.

Let's illustrate the six operations with the same case. For example, "sending roses to the beloved one on Valentine's Day" (focus on product):

- Substitute it: sending lemons on Valentine's Day.
- Invert it: sending roses all the days of the year *except* on Valentine's Day.
- Combine it: sending roses + pencil on Valentine's Day.
- Exaggerate it: sending dozens of roses on Valentine's Day (upward exaggeration) or sending only one rose on Valentine's Day (downward exaggeration).
- Eliminate it: not sending roses on Valentine's Day.
- Reorder it: the beloved sending roses to an admirer on Valentine's Day.

All the operations have triggered nonlogical phrases. They seem absurd. Their apparent uselessness comes from the fact that all of them have generated a gap. Yet if you have been able to generate a gap, you are halfway to doing lateral marketing.

These six operations can be applied at any of the three levels. So once a product or service has been chosen and a focus has been defined, you only have to select one of the six strategies and apply it to your focus to generate a gap.

Let's see six examples at each one of the levels:

Market Level

- Substitution of a situation: popcorn in discos instead of in cinemas.
- Inversion of an occasion: roses to send when couples have quarreled.
- Combination of targets: champagne for both parents and kids.
- Exaggeration of utility: a pencil that never is used up.
- Elimination of utility: a car that cannot run.
- Reordering a utility:[5] "a writer, then a reader" into "a reader, then a writer."

Product Level

- Substitution: hot dog with a cookie instead of a hot dog roll.
- Inversion: pizza that is not delivered.
- Combination: pen with car's fuel level indicator.
- Exaggeration: bottle containing 200 liters of Coke.
- Elimination: laptop without a screen.
- Reordering: developing a photo film after having seen the photos.

---

[5]Reordering is a difficult technique to apply at the market level, since it requires two or more items to be reordered, while the market level focus implies choosing *one* item (situation, time, occasion, utility, or target). Reordering is much easier to apply at the product level or mix level.

Marketing Mix Level

- Substitution (price): paying for diapers with a bank loan.
- Inversion (price): shops without prices on the products.
- Combination (channel): buying gasoline from kiosks and gas stations together.
- Exaggeration (postsale service): a painting the customer always returns after buying.
- Elimination (communication): clothes with no advertising or brand.
- Reordering (payment modality): paying for phone calls before making them.

Observe that all the techniques provoke inconsistencies. This is the result of having applied a movement based on a technique that does not use logical thinking.

The second step is to do a lateral displacement on one of the three levels. There are six techniques for doing lateral displacements: substitution, inversion, combination, exaggeration, elimination, and reordering.

Similarities between Lateral Displacements and Brainstorming Techniques Brainstorming techniques have some aspects in common with lateral thinking, but they are not the same in all respects.

Lateral displacements and brainstorming have in common that for a period of time judgment is interrupted. Typical phrases of brainstorming session directors are that "everything is valid now" or "it is forbidden to judge." A lateral displacement also implies judgment interruption, because logical thinking is deliberately interrupted.

The differences are:

- Brainstorming sessions always involve groups, whereas lateral displacements can be done either individually or in groups.
- The brainstorming session is a technique for generating a high number of ideas, whereas the lateral displacement consists of introducing only *one* possibility inside a sequence.
- In brainstorming sessions, there is often a lack of concrete techniques for generating gaps. In lateral marketing the six techniques provide direction.
- Making connections is not always a part of brainstorming sessions. Without this operation, the lateral creative process is not finished.

How to Identify Whether We Are Doing Lateral or Vertical Marketing The main distinction between lateral and vertical marketing is the presence or absence of a gap when doing a lateral displacement. For example, if we try to do a lateral displacement with the attribute "fast" for cars, there is no gap to be solved. If we use the attribute "low fuel consumption" there is no gap. If we try to do a lateral displacement with the attribute "heavy consumers" for purchasers of

119

cheese, there is no gap (see Figure 6.12). Absence of gap means that we are using vertical, not lateral thinking. We are simply breaking a given market or product into parts.

> *The way to determine whether we are doing lateral or vertical marketing is by checking if we have a gap in front of us or not. The absence of a gap implies that we are working an innovation into the same market or category.*

6.5.4   Step 3: Making Connections

At this stage, some people may think that generating illogical stimuli is a waste of time. But the point of doing a displacement is to *apply logic with more strength than ever.*

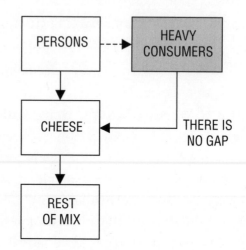

Figure 6.12   Absence of Gap Indicates Vertical Thinking

A stimulus is just a stimulus, and we will throw it away once the gap has been solved. If you insist on conserving the stimulus (e.g., apples for consumption by companies) you will never solve it. The stimulus is like extracting essence of perfume from flower petals. We squeeze them, obtain some extracts, and then throw away the petals. Very little perfume essence is extracted from a petal, but a few drops of extract are enough for a bottle of perfume.

In the same way, the stimulus has to be analyzed to extract valuable pieces of information.

For extracting the value, we must do a valuation. This is not saying what is good or bad, logical or illogical, positive or negative, useful or useless. Rather, it consists of extracting only valid conclusions and observations from our stimulus.

In order to do a valuation, there are three possible techniques.

First Valuation Technique: Follow the Buying Process of the Stimulus Step by Step   Here, we need to imagine the whole purchase process of the stimulus generated, from the need identification until the postbuying behavior, passing through the information gathering process, the decision making, the usage of the product, and so on.

We should imagine a hypothetical buyer going through the whole process and making a "history" out of it.

In each step, we should write down every valuable idea or characteristic of the stimulus, as well as the possible improvements that could make our "history" more real.

For example, earlier we proposed popcorn for discos.

121

Valuation Let's imagine a couple in the disco: They order popcorn, but have difficulty seeing it because it is dark (idea: popcorn in discos could be colored with fluorescent colorants). They sit down at a table, eat, and now feel thirsty. So they order drinks (utility: eating popcorn provokes thirst; we could sell more drinks if we offer free popcorn).

Connection Thus we have solved the gap. The opportunity for popcorn companies would be to convince discos to offer free popcorn placed on tables or at the bar. People would eat popcorn and would feel more thirsty. The profit margin of an additional drink compensates for nearly four and a half pounds of popcorn. Popcorn would be made fluorescent by sprinkling colored salt on it.

Second Valuation Technique: Extract the Utilities and the Positive Things Here we search for positive aspects in our impossible stimulus. We can afterward forget the stimulus and propose an alternative way to produce those positive effects.

Let's take the example of the painting that the customer always returns.

Valuation What will be the positive effects of customers never being happy with the painting they bought? They would have to bring it back and the gallery would have to return their money. This would be a negative effect, so let's discard that. Another effect: They could exchange it and have a different painting in their living room. This is positive, because they would have paid for only one painting.

122

Let's take that positive idea: paying for only one painting, but having the possibility to change it every time. Now, forget about the stimulus and think of a way of producing this.

Connection   A new service to be offered by galleries: renting paintings.

- Target: those who are not that much focused on property ownership but on its utility as decoration.
- Need: changing your paintings each six months for free.
- Use: paintings as decoration, not as property.
- Product: a service of choosing a painting each six months.
- Price: You pay the cost of a painting, but do not own it. You just have the right to use it for a period of time. Each six months you gain equity, and after 10 years, the mortgage is finished. Then you can choose a painting and keep it.
- Channel: galleries, banks.
- Communication: advertising campaigns.
- Message: pay for one painting, use 20 before making a final choice.

Third Valuation Technique: Find a Possible Setting
Find a possible setting (environment, people you may be with, place, time, occasion) where the stimulus could make some sense.

Then, move or transform the stimulus as much as you need to take it to that setting.

Let's take the example of the roses to be sent when couples have had a quarrel and do not talk to each other.

123

Valuation One situation where sending the roses would make sense is if one of them (normally, the male) wants to apologize. Then, sending roses would indicate that he is sorry and wants to make peace.

Connection It would be necessary that we have a specific accepted communication code. So, consumer education through a campaign would be required. In order to differentiate the occasion from the one of Valentine's Day, we could sell the idea that five white roses represent the five letters of "s-o-r-r-y." If everyone knew this, each couple would buy once or twice per year five white roses (in addition to those given on Valentine's Day). This is an instance of incremental volume.

Making connections is not easy, but it is not terribly difficult, either. It is a matter of practice, some training, and a very positive attitude in observing your stimulus.

In order to prove it, one possible connection is given next for the rest of the 18 examples on pages 117 and 118.

Market Level

- *Combination of targets: champagne for both parents and kids.* The connection could be false champagne made of apple juice, with no alcohol, but with fizz. The brand is the same, but the bottle is smaller. Parents drink real champagne from the big one and give kids fizzy apple juice.
- *Exaggeration of utility: a pencil that never is used up.* This was the origin of the idea of the mechanical pencils we replace carbon lead in.

124

- *Elimination of utility: a car that cannot run*. This was the origin of driving simulators.
- *Reordering a utility: books made by readers*. Hundreds of people could each write one page (one after another). Every additional page would be put on the Internet on a web site. Visitors would vote whether the new page is to be approved. The resulting novel would have thousands of readers before being launched.

Product Level

- *Substitution: hot dog with a cookie instead of a hot dog roll*. The connection could be a type of funny afternoon snack for kids. Biscuits with chocolate inside, imitating all types of sandwiches: hot dog, hamburger, ham and cheese.
- *Inversion: pizza that is not delivered*. That was the origin of the idea of refrigerated pizza, a new product that in Spain has reduced the home pizza delivery business by 30 percent.
- *Combination: pen with car's fuel indicator*. This would lead to the idea of a pen with marks for indicating when there is ink for only three, two, or one additional hour of writing.
- Exaggeration: *bottle containing 200 liters of Coke*. Coca-Cola could reach an agreement with refrigerator manufacturers to install a button inside the refrigerator (like the ones you press with a glass and ice water comes out). Water would be merged with Coke essence (like in soda fountains and bars). This would be ideal for heavy Coke consumers and much cheaper. For Coca-Cola, the benefit would be that brand loyalty would be ensured—during the whole life of the refrigerator!

125

- *Elimination: laptop without a screen.* To be used in places where someone has a table screen, it would be a good way of carrying the processor and the files (cheaper and less weight). It would not be valid for mobility occasions, but would be for people who have several working places (office, university, home) in the same city.

- *Reordering: the idea of developing a photo after seeing it.* This led to the idea of the photo contacts service, where a customer can ask only for the film to be developed in a very small size (in half a page it is possible to see all the photos of one film). Once the person (or customer) sees each image, he or she orders normal size for the ones that are worth enough.

Marketing Mix Level

- *Substitution (price): paying for diapers with a bank loan.* All baby needs are charged to you when the child is five years old (with interest). This would help many people to have kids, because they would have time to save money.

- *Inversion (price): shops without prices on the products.* A company could build a service based on obtaining updated information about prices of the same items in similar shops in town. Automatically it puts the lowest price on its merchandise. This would be a warranty for consumers who would know without browsing that shops with that service have the lowest prices.

- *Combination (channel): buying gasoline from kiosks and gas stations together.* Gasoline distribution companies could sell tickets you can use to pay in gas stations or insert in gas pumps. These tickets could be bought in kiosks.

- *Elimination (communication): clothes with no advertising or brand.* This is aimed at people against globalization and multinationals. If there is a "no logo" ticket, it means that the profit margin goes to undeveloped countries that manufactured the clothing.

- *Reordering: paying before calling.* This is the origin of pre-paid calling cards (cellular or fixed phones).

Of course not all of these are clear business opportunities. Some may be. Some may need a few adjustments to be considered seriously. And any idea should be adequately tested before launch.

It would not be justified to say that lateral marketing is not useful because it produces a lot of useless ideas. Just a few ideas have to be winners.

The third step is to connect or solve the gap. The way to do it is by valuating, rather than evaluating. There are three valuation techniques: following the purchase process, extracting the positive, and finding a setting.

6.6 Final Outputs of the Lateral Marketing Process

There are three types of outputs in a lateral marketing process:

1. *Same product, new utility*. Effect: expansion of the vertical marketing area (e.g., roses for apologizing, apples on reception desks). (See Figure 6.13.)

2. *New product, new utility*. Effect: creation of a new market or category (e.g., fluorescent popcorn, kids' champagne). (See Figure 6.14.)

3. *New product, same utility*. Effect: creation of a new subcategory (e.g., prepaid cards). (See Figure 6.15.)

The final outcome of a lateral marketing process can be a new utility for the same product, a new category, or a new subcategory.

6.7 Examples from Chapter 4 under the Lateral Marketing Framework

Now that a framework has been proposed, we can wonder where all the lateral marketing innovations described in Chapter 4 came from.[6] We apply lateral marketing to the following examples:

- Cereal bars are obtained by placing cereals in a snacking occasion in the street (focus: occasion; displacement technique: substitution).

---

[6]Only the person or people who had the idea really know the source, but we are trying to propose a formal process for arriving at the same or similar ideas.

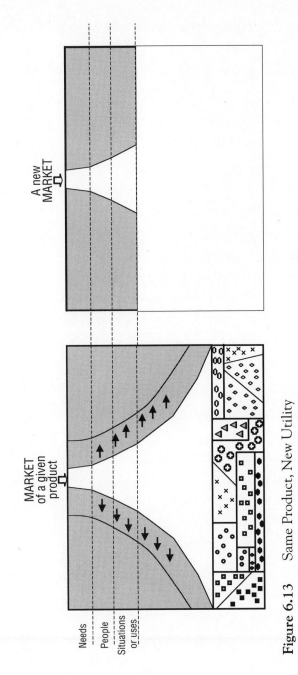

Figure 6.13 Same Product, New Utility

129

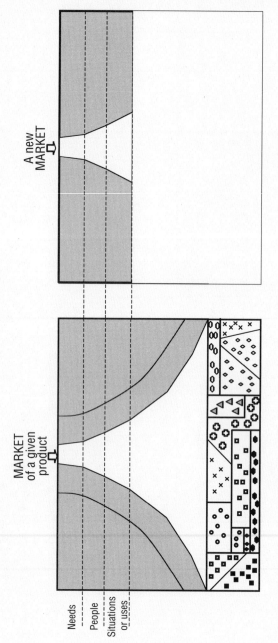

Figure 6.14 New Product, New Utility

130

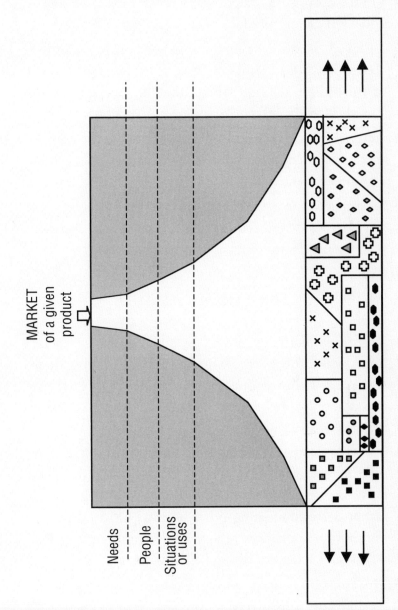

MARKET
of a given
product

Needs

People

Situations
or uses

Figure 6.15 New Product, Same Utility

131

- Kinder Surprise is obtained by combining a chocolate and a gift (focus: product; technique: combination).

- 7-Eleven Japan becoming a depot for Internet-purchased items is obtained by inverting the main activity of the shops: selling. "Shops that do not sell" is the stimulus (focus: service; technique: inversion).

- Actimel from Dannon is obtained by adding the need for bacteria protection to the one of eating (focus: need; technique: combination).

- Supermarkets in gas stations are obtained by putting food stores in a different setting: gas stations (focus: situation; technique: substitution).

- Cyber cafés are obtained by combining two products: cafés and computers (focus: product; technique: combination).

- "Be the godfather of a kid" is obtained by exaggerating downward the service under "sale": gathering donations for helping one person instead of gathering donations for helping a community (focus: service; technique: exaggeration).

- The "Big Brother" contest is obtained as a result of exaggerating upward many aspects of a contest: a contest that lasts six months with around-the-clock broadcasts, together with eliminating other aspects: no conductor of the show, no quizzes or tests to be passed (focus: product; techniques: exaggeration and elimination).

- The Pull-Ups concept is obtained from proposing an impossible target, by inverting its characteristics: diapers for

132

kids above two years old instead of below two years old (focus: target group; technique: inversion).

- Barbie is obtained (according to the explanation of Ruth Handler) from substituting the experiential utility (psychological need) of girls (focus: utility; technique: substitution).

- Walkman is obtained from proposing putting audio players in an impossible setting—walking in the street or any other mobility occasion (focus: place; technique: substitution).

Lateral Marketing at the Market Level

T his chapter gives practical recommendations on how to apply lateral marketing at the market level by using one simple technique: change one of the dimensions.

7.1   Change of Dimension as the Most Practical Technique

Even though there are six techniques for doing lateral displacements at the market level, we recommend substitution as the most efficient and easy-to-use method.

The reason is that the market level contains several dimensions where a product or service competes. These dimensions are need, target, and occasion. This last dimension is a combination of: place, time, situation, and experience.

$$Market = Need, \ target, \ \overbrace{place, \ time, \ situation, \ experience}^{Occasion}$$

No single product or service can exist without considering these dimensions. Therefore, operations such as "eliminating a dimension," "reordering a dimension," "combining two dimensions," and "exaggerating a dimension" would require some effort.[1]

On the other hand, substituting a dimension for another one is easy (e.g., cereals to be taken in the street instead of at home and cereals to be eaten at night instead of in the morning).

The method "change of dimension" consists of substituting one of the dimensions of the market for another that is discarded.

7.2 Dimensions to Be Changed: Concept and Examples

Here are some examples for each of the dimensions.[2]

7.2.1 Changing the Need: Trying to Cover Another Utility

This dimension consists of selecting a need we are not covering and thinking about how the product should be in order to meet that need.

---

[1]See examples of these operations at the market level in Chapter 6.
[2]In Chapters 7 to 9, all the lateral displacements are italicized.

138

Here are several examples:

- Red Bull opened the category today called energy drinks—*soft drinks that stimulate one's energy.* This serves a new need besides the normal one of quenching thirst.

- Wonderbra added to normal bras the need of certain women who would like to *appear more voluptuous.*

- Digital alarms companies added the function of storing the hours in which alarms are switched on and off as *a way of controlling* when external *staff* opens or closes a shop.

- Telephone taxi companies, trying to find additional volume, started using *taxis as couriers.* Business-to-business companies such as advertising agencies tend to order very urgent local deliveries. There is always a taxi ready, whereas couriers sometimes require some time to pick up the package, given fleet capacity limitations. By adding to taxis the utility of transporting packages instead of transporting people, the market was expanded.

- A TV music contest used *CDs as a way of voting.* CDs of the participants were recorded and launched in music shops. The winner of the contest was the one with the highest sales among all participants. The audience was asked to buy their preferred participant recording as a way of voting for him or her instead of traditional methods, such as sending an SMS (short message service) or voting through the telephone.

- Bayer aspirin has found many competitors in acetaminophen-based medicines, which are used to reduce aches. Bayer is communicating on TV that *aspirin*, apart from aches, is also good *for preventing heart attacks*. The commercial recommends taking one each day for such a prevention. The new utility is bringing additional volume and brand loyalty.

7.2.2 Changing the Target: A Person, Persons, or a Group

Substituting a person or group consists of choosing someone who is a nonpotential target of the product or service.

The nonpotential targets are the ones who are not likely to buy or use a product or service. They should not be confused with the potential target definition, which refers to the people who are not buying now but who have the need the product covers, so they can become customers at any moment. The potential target is already included in the vertical marketing process with the current target definition.

The diapers example in Chapter 4 is a perfect instance: diapers for children above three years old—Pull-Ups. But there are other examples of products that were altered in order to reach nonpotential targets:

- Gillette started selling *razors to women* through Gillette Venus, a pink and feminine razor designed especially for women's legs.

- A French cheese manufacturer made it possible for *children to eat cheese* as a dessert through Kidiboo, a sweetened and creamy cheese on a stick, so it can be eaten as if it was an ice cream. Kids love it. They would normally refuse to eat a pure piece of cheese.

- *Amusement parks* generated the idea of offering these locations during the weekdays of winter, when there is a low attendance, to companies *for sales conferences*. After the conference, colleagues would share a fun-filled free day in the park. An important additional source of business was generated.

- Singing accompanied by an orchestra was limited to professionals, but many people love to sing. Karaoke was an invention for enabling *any person to sing with orchestral accompaniment*.

- *Classical music for babies* has led to the recent success of the videos "Baby Mozart" and "Baby Beethoven" where the composers' main compositions are played with images.

- An idea: State authorities film road conditions in order to control traffic. The change of dimension would consist of *showing the road conditions on TV*, so that citizens can decide whether to wait before leaving their homes or to change routes. State authorities could charge for this service.

A very powerful technique for identifying nonpotential users or buyers is to think about the barriers to buying or consuming the product. Removing the purchasing barriers can lead to new consumers and sales.

7.2.3 Changing the Time: Choosing New Moments

This dimension consists of choosing new moments of buying, usage, or consumption of a company's offering.

Many products are strongly embedded into specific moments. Orange juice is for breakfast. A whiskey is consumed after dinner or when talking with friends. The same people having lunch may order a martini or vermouth.

Part of a lateral marketer's job is to detect new moments to imbed the product.

Here are examples:

- Opencor is a new concept of small *supermarkets that are open at night.* They cater to professional women who work late in the evening and have no time for shopping during the day.

- Hotels have been able to *rent rooms during the afternoon* in addition to overnight. This has occurred in some Mediterranean and Caribbean countries, where siesta, after having lunch, is common, especially on weekends. The hotel offers two hours of room usage for sleeping if the customer has had lunch in the hotel restaurant, regardless of whether he or she is a hotel guest.

- A wholesaler developed *delivery services during the night.* The idea was to offer five-minute deliveries from midnight onward, when pubs and bars are open and running out of product is a problem. It was the only wholesaler who was distributing bottles during the night. The price was much higher than usual.

There are many moments that are still waiting to be owned by products. Coffee usually is consumed in the morning. Many people like to drink it at night, but even decaffeinated coffee prevents them from sleeping. There could be a clear opportunity for a *"before going to bed"* coffee *that will not interfere with sleeping.*

7.2.4 Changing the Place: Move Your Product into a New Setting

This is one of the easiest substitution techniques to use, and it gives good results.

This dimension consists of choosing places of purchase, usage, or consumption where the product or service cannot be present now.

It is interesting to observe how some products are strongly linked to certain places. Popcorn is for cinemas, peanuts are for airplanes, and so on.

The opportunity is to propose an "impossible" place or setting for the product as a way of thinking about how to change the normal place.

Here are some examples:

- Global Positioning System technology was conceived for ships and boats. If we place *GPS in a car*, we obtain a new service for recovering stolen cars or for finding the location of a destination.

- Commercials were traditionally placed at the beginning and end of programs. Placing *an ad in the middle of a program* led to the idea of "product placement" as a new way of advertising, namely exhibiting brands as part of a TV show or movie.

- *Mobile phones inside home alarm systems* have been a way of foiling thieves who might cut regular telephone lines. Now this connection is done through wireless phones.

- *Apples at a reception desk* are a way of welcoming someone—a new use for apples, apart from eating them.

- *Home cinema* consists of placing all the special effects of cinemas (Dolby surround sound, horizontal screen) inside people's homes. Of course, a full range of new products had to be developed for it.

- *The idea of hotels in the countryside* is a lateral displacement that generated the new tourism concept—"rural tourism." Old rural houses have been restored and prepared to be small and quiet hotels of no more than a dozen rooms for people looking for a quiet rest.

- Nestea is a soft drink designed to facilitate *drinking cold or iced tea outside of the home*. This lateral marketing innovation involved a joint venture between Nestlé and the Coca-Cola Company, the former for producing, the latter for distributing.

Lateral marketing can sometimes require choosing a partner, because it may require technologies that companies lack. For example, education is being combined with entertainment in a new discipline: eductainment, which requires combined efforts of organizations that previously had not worked together. As another example, pharmaceuticals are finding a better source of innovation in biotechnology. This forces the two industries to work together to create new products.

7.2.5 Changing the Occasion: Link Your Product to an Event

Occasions and events are often linked to specific products. Champagne is for Christmas, end-of-year parties, or celebrations; white wine is for a special dinner; candy is for Halloween; cake is for birthdays; roses for Valentine's Day.

The challenge for marketers is to propose events or occasions where the product is not considered now.

- UNICEF was able to capitalize on the occasion of *wishing Merry Christmas* or Happy New Year by mail. UNICEF greeting cards help others and at the same time send best wishes to relatives and friends.
- For example, Frito-Lay launched Doritos in the United States first with sauce and afterward, flavored. In contrast, Frito-Lay in Europe first sold flavored and only recently with sauce, under the brand Dippas. All the advertising

was concentrated in *showing teenagers meeting* at a friend's house. Embedding Dippas into this occasion allowed the product to act as a food substitute. Frito-Lay gained a high incremental volume by situating the product in a nontypical salty snacks occasion.

- The Oscar statue is a sign of recognition in the film industry. *Plastic Oscar statues* have been marketed with the meaning of congratulating someone for a personal success, such as obtaining a diploma or winning a competition.

7.2.6 Changing the Activity: Place Products into Experiences

This dimension consists of choosing activities or experiences where other products are strongly positioned but not the one being considered.

Here are examples:

- Wanting to increase the size of the fruit market, a Spanish company has tried to link fruit to the activity of practicing sport. This company has installed vending machines with *oranges, bananas, and apples in gyms* and fitness clubs. Now many people eat a piece of fruit to recover energy after practicing sport.
- An important radio station wanted to launch a news program but had difficulty finding new targets or needs. The

solution was to relate the program to a concrete activity: *News for listening in the car* when someone is driving a short distance. The solution was a 24-hour program with 30-minute overviews of all the day's news. If you are going to be in the car for at least 30 minutes, tuning in to this station ensures that you will be completely informed. This radio station is today's leader in the category of radio "information" programs.

- *Placing the activity of taking risks into practicing sports* has led to the recent "extreme sports," such as bungee jumping and skydiving.
- Many people spend a lot of the time in the car. *Language courses on audiotapes* are thought ideal to be listened to while spending time in traffic jams.

7.3 Connecting the Product with the New Dimension

After a lateral displacement has been made using the "change of dimension" technique we will face a product or service in a new setting.

The change of dimension has provoked a gap between the product and service and a new dimension.

To connect the gap, the best approach is to follow the purchase/consumption process step-by-step. Why? Because it clearly identifies the lacking elements, the product elements to be removed, and the product elements to be maintained in connecting the product to the new dimension.

In some cases, it will be possible to keep the product as it is. But in most cases, it will be necessary to change it. Let's illustrate both cases.

7.3.1 Connections Made without Altering the Product

The only way of not changing the physical product is by finding the utility that allows it to be placed in the new dimension.

For example, apples do not have to be changed when they are put at a reception desk. Nor does fruit placed in a vending machine in a gym need to be changed. But we do need to communicate a new meaning in each case. Apples create a welcoming effect; fruit carry the meaning of restoring energy.

After changing the dimension, if we do not want to change the product, we must seek a new utility for it and communicate it.

7.3.2 Connections Made by Altering the Product

In most cases, we will have to redefine some characteristics of the product. We will identify elements to be removed. Those are the elements that are anchoring the product to its natural dimension.

There are only two ways of handling these anchors: by eliminating them or by changing them.

Here are examples:

- If we wanted to obtain the sound effects of cinemas in a home video appliance, the main anchor is the power capacity of television baffles. It is not possible to convince people to change their TVs. This problem was solved by providing two external baffles to be connected to the TV. Additionally, baffles could be placed behind the viewers in order to provide surround sound effects throughout the room.

- In the case of Kidiboo, the anchors were that kids did not find cheese to be sweet or fun to eat. These anchors were removed by adding a sugar to cheese and by inserting a stick into the cheese in order to imitate an ice cream.

- In the case of Wonderbra, the main anchor in the need to appear more voluptuous was the lack of volume in a regular bra. This was easily solved by using a thicker cloth for manufacturing the product.

Anchors are the product elements that do not let us get into the new dimension. We must change or eliminate them.

7.4 A Complete Case: Proposing a New Business Concept

The previous examples in this chapter correspond to products and services that already exist. We would like to show a complete process for proposing a new product that does not exist today.

We thought that it would be a challenge to think of a service that allowed Internet purchasing by people who do not own a computer. Here it is:

- *Service:* Online shopping.
- *Lateral marketing technique:* change of target.
- *New dimension through changing the target:* The displacement is to visualize people without computers buying through the Internet.
- *Gap:* Someone who does not have a computer cannot buy through the Internet.
- *Technique for closing the gap:* Finding a setting where the connection is possible and imagining the usage process.
- *Possible setting:* We could think of an outlet full of computers connected to the Internet. Customers can enter the shop and use computers for online shopping.
- *Identified anchors:* The consumer lacks surfing experience and does not know portals for online shopping. Delivery points need to be specified. Not everyone may have a credit card for paying. People may just surf the Internet without purchasing.
- *Ways to weigh anchors:* In the outlet specialized clerks coach users. There is a list of recommended portals organized by categories. The software is programmed to allow visiting only e-commerce portals. There is the

possibility of collecting and paying for purchased goods in the outlet.

Service name: Cyber-Shops. Result of connecting the gap: additional volume for e-commerce.

7.5   Ancillary Techniques for Displacing the Market Level

We have illustrated the technique of "substitution" and called it "change of dimension." But we said that there are five additional techniques for making lateral displacements.

We recommend using these other techniques once a marketing professional has acquired more experience with the "change of dimension" technique. The reason is that the operations of inverting, combining, exaggerating, eliminating, and reordering require more effort than when working with the dimensions of the market definition (i.e., need, target, place, time, situation, experience).

Nevertheless, here are some examples.

7.5.1   *Combining the Dimension "Place"*

Using the same telephone for home and out of home. This lateral displacement led Viag Interkom, an important German telecom operator, to a new communication concept. It offered a mobile solution which, by detecting the antenna that was receiving the signal of the user, could identify whether the customer was at home. This allowed the company to charge the same price per minute as for a fixed phone when the person was at home. In this way, the telecom company could capture additional traffic and also convince many people to have only one phone instead of two. The product was called Homezone.

7.5.2 Reordering the Dimension "Time"

Welcoming a guest before arriving at the hotel. This lateral displacement led to the idea of placing a hotel employee in the airport who helps guests by taking their luggage to the taxi, giving the room number and keys to the customers, and telling the taxi driver the hotel's name and address. These tasks are tedious for travelers who arrive in an unknown country. This reception gives security and good help. This was not expected by guests. This service increased "repeat purchase loyalty" rates by 30 percent. Cost was zero dollars (it was provided by the regular hotel staff).

7.5.3 Exaggerating the Dimension "Place"

A mobile phone with worldwide coverage. This lateral displacement led a company to attempt development of mobile services through satellite technology. This service would allow this brand's mobile phone to be used even in the middle of a desert. It would also eliminate paying for roaming services. (However, this Iridium project was temporarily canceled due to its cost.) The same brand provides line access to all countries.

Another example of place and time exaggerations together led to the popular transportation concept called "Inter-rail." It consists of *a single train ticket, valid for the entire month of August on all European trains.* It is addressed to young people who travel in summer all around Europe.

7.5.4 Inverting the Dimension "Need"

A book that cannot be read. Books are used by many people as decorative objects. Shelves of houses need to be filled with books, and some time ago a new concept was launched: empty books with no more utility than decorating shelves of houses.

The product consists of an empty box decorated as a book with a very luxurious look. There are even series of 10 or more books together. Fake books have also been used with new uses, such as hiding objects or keeping the remains of a relative who was cremated.

7.5.5 Inverting the Dimension "Target"

A turnabout in the electricity sector. Customers generating and distributing energy for the energy company led to a business concept under development in some European countries concerned about natural energy systems: houses with solar panels in their roofs that generate enough energy for the houses, with the remaining energy being sold to the energy distributor company.

7.5.6 Eliminating the Dimension "Time"

A game with no dimension of time. This lateral displacement led to the idea of role games—games with no specific duration and where players adopt a given role or a given protagonist. Role games have become very popular among young people and even adults and have easily been translated to the Internet.

Lateral Marketing
at the Product Level

T his chapter gives practical recommendations on how to apply lateral marketing at the product level by using the six techniques for making lateral displacements.

8.1   Philosophy behind Applying Lateral Marketing at the Product Level

We are going to change something in the product or service, and then we will ask: "What can it be used for?" "In which situations might this product be valid?" "Which target would like this idea?"

We will have to find a utility, target, or setting for the product that was altered. But there is no assurance that we will find it: This is a probabilistic process.

Then why should marketers dedicate time to it? The reason is that most innovations have appeared as a result of a coincidence.[1]

---

[1]The examples of Velcro, Morse, and Goodyear can be found with more detail in *Cracking Creativity: The Secrets of Creative Genius*, by Michael Michalko (Berkeley, CA: Ten Speed Press, 1998).

For example, the Swiss inventor George de Mestral was out hunting one day when he had difficulty removing thistle burrs from his clothes. When he arrived home, he put the burrs under a microscope, and observed the way the hooks had been linked to his clothes. This led to his invention of Velcro.

In working to develop the long-distance telegraph, Samuel Morse solved a problem with his famous communication system when he saw travelers changing horses to continue traveling. He related this concept to the one of giving regular impulses of power to signals traveling along the telegraph wire.

Charles Goodyear was trying to obtain a rubber that would be easier to manipulate. By error, he poured a mixture that became too hard, but still could be used. He discovered the vulcanization process, which allowed the manufacture of rubber tires, among other rubber products.

Many companies have encountered a sudden competitor who, by taking their product and changing something, introduced a real threat. Sweets manufacturers were surprised when lollipops were launched as the first sweet with a stick inserted in it. Then, traditional sweets executives asked: "How is it possible that we didn't think of this first? It was right in front of us and we never saw it!"

By considering many ways to alter the product or service, we will likely discover a few creative ideas.

Someone at 3M showed a paper bearing a poorly performing glue to other colleagues and asked whether they had any ideas on what it could be used for. Someone proposed using it to stick on pages. The Post-it concept was born and created a new category; it became one of the biggest marketing successes. So we should not underestimate random search.

8.2 Dissection of the Product

In lateral marketing at a market level we use dimensions (Chapter 7). At the product level, we use pieces that result from the product dissection. Remember that products are a result of isolated elements that someone organized in a given way. We must decompose the product again in order to change it.

For example, a "pen" could be split into: ink, color, plastic cap, plastic body.

One interesting way to organize the elements or pieces of a product is by using the main levels of the product:[2]

- Tangible product or service.[3]
- Packaging (if applicable).
- Brand attributes.
- Usage or purchase.

After splitting the object into pieces, we must remove or change some of them. The way to change pieces is by

---

[2]The core benefit is not included in this list because it has already been covered within the utility/need dimension of the market level.

[3]Tangible product or service can also be organized into three parts: the main product, the increased product, and the potential product. See Philip Kotler, *Marketing Management*, 11th edition (Upper Saddle River, NJ: Prentice Hall, 2003).

applying a lateral displacement to one or several of the pieces (elements).

8.3   Selecting the Entry Doors

But which elements should we choose as entry points once the product has been split? There are two possibilities here: natural anchors or other elements.

8.3.1   *Selecting Natural Anchors as Entry Points*

We use the term "anchors" to refer to the product elements we have to remove in order to imagine a new idea. We will use the term "natural anchors" for the product elements that become essential in order to recognize the product.

For example, in a notebook, pages are a natural anchor because a notebook without pages will hardly be recognized as a notebook. Another anchor would be that the pages must somehow be linked to each other. Notebook covers, though, are not a natural anchor. We could remove the cover and still have a notebook.

Selecting natural anchors as entry points for applying any of the six techniques helps us move away from the product because we are modifying its essence.

8.3.2   *Selecting Other Elements as Entry Points*

Alternatively, we can select any other element as an entry point. In this case, we will have more chance to create a subcategory rather than a new category because we will be altering elements that are not essential in recognizing the product.

For example, if we decide to modify the metal rings that join the notebook's pages, we may come up with staples or other systems. We will have a new subcategory, and it would still be a notebook.[4]

8.4 Applying Lateral Displacements: Concept and Examples

After having dissected the product and selected specific elements as entry points, we need to provoke a lateral displacement. At the product level, the six techniques introduced in Chapter 6 have an easy application. Each of these six lateral displacement techniques will be here defined and several examples will also be listed.

8.4.1 *Substitution*

Substitution consists of removing one/several elements of the product and changing it/them. It also consists of imitating aspects of other products.

Tangible Product or Service *Substituting "students teach students" for "professors teach students" has led to an interesting*

---

[4]These rules may have exceptions, depending on how connections are finally made in order to solve the gap.

educational approach. Students, one by one, prepare a class. Every day, one of them explains a lesson to the rest. The professor acts as a moderator of the class. Rates of attention and teenagers' motivation are boosted.

Changing watch clockwork mechanisms by using batteries led to a new category of watches and, later on, to digital watches.

Substituting the backing of a carpet (normally made of synthetics or rope) with the same cloth as the upper part led to the new concept of two-sided carpets with different designs on each side.

Substituting the same car complements in different car brands has allowed important cost reductions, which have been translated into price reductions.

Packaging   Removing glass or plastic as the material used for milk containers and using cartons instead led to the Tetrabrik concept, by Tetra-pak.

Brand Attributes[5]   Removing the attribute "cute" from baby shoes and changing it to "fashionable" has led Nike to expand its business into the baby shoes market.

Shampoo and soap were intended to be soft, perfumed, elegant, with low acid so as not to irritate the eyes. After Sara Lee's marketing team in the cosmetics division observed that

---

[5]For doing a lateral displacement through the brand attributes, we must use characteristics that have nothing to do with our product (for example, fast yogurts); otherwise we would just be applying the positioning strategies of a vertical marketing process.

the attribute "healthy" was becoming important in many food categories, Sanex gel was created, giving a name to the new category of healthy soaps and shampoos. The brand opened the new axis of health in the positioning maps of the market.

"Intelligent buildings" are a new category of construction where modern systems of control, security, and automation are installed.

Usage or Purchase Inserting a regular stick into a candy created lollipops for children. This meant a substitution of the way of consumption, which created a revolution in the sweets market.

8.4.2 Combination

Combination consists of adding one or several elements to the product or service, maintaining the rest.

Tangible Product or Service *Motorbike + roof* led to the concept C1 of BMW, which opened a new category in the transportation market.

Pedals + electricity = "Pedelec," a bicycle with electric batteries that are recharged by the bicycle being ridden. In upward slopes, when pedals detect an extra effort, the battery is automatically activated and the rider is helped by the motor. In downward slopes, batteries get charged again. The effort of the rider is always the same. Result: one million units already sold in China.

163

An idea: *An airplane with rooms* like a train would lead to the idea of an exclusive transoceanic flight service for very few passengers who have their own private room inside the plane. Name: air lit service.

Packaging Fitting spigots into caps of five-liter water bottles has allowed consumers to place the bottles lying down inside the refrigerator and to use the cap as a tap. People open the refrigerator, turn the cap, and water flows. This avoids having to lift the heavy five-liter bottles.

Brand Attributes By *adding the attribute "funny" to ties* (which are supposed to be serious), the subcategory of funny ties with Walt Disney or Looney Tunes characters was created. Even executives wear them in their regular professional activities.

Usage or Purchase By *adding "listening" to the reading of a book*, the books-on-tape category was created.

8.4.3 Inversion

Inversion consists of saying the contrary or adding "no" to one/several element(s) of the product or service.

Tangible Product or Service Just-cooked pizza changed into *non-just-cooked pizza* led to the idea of frozen and refrigerated pizzas, which created additional markets for pizza manufacturers.[6]

The inversion of the contracting concept: *an employee with whom we do not sign a contract* leads to the concept of the part-time worker. Companies now can rent part-time workers to handle peak volume periods.

Packaging   Ketchup is thick, and this implies waiting for the product to flow down in the bottle before pouring it on the food. Several companies thought of *inverting the ketchup bottle* and putting the cap in the bottom. Ketchup is always ready to flow out when opening the bottle.

Brand Attributes   *Pen with writing that does not last* led to the idea of Velleda, the famous marking pen used to write on plastic whose writing can easily be deleted with the hand.

Usage or Purchase   *Lottery with no raffle* led to the idea of self-administered lottery tickets where someone scratches a piece of paper and the prize appears directly on it. There are no numbers anymore.

Cinematography gives viewers the effect of moving photographs. Inverting it, we obtain *still photographs observed by people who are moving*. One setting where this is possible is a

---

[6]It is interesting to observe that pizza home delivery companies have always discarded the precooked pizzas as their business. They have been worried about the image consequences of selling precooked pizzas under the same brand as delivered ones. This could be overcome with appropriate communication campaigns, so this is a symptom of the reluctance of companies to change their market definition, as explained in Chapter 2.

train. The system is being tested in the New York subway system. The different images of an ad are painted on the walls of tunnels. The idea is that when travelling inside the subway train and looking through the windows, one would see the same effect as in a cinema!

An interesting concept appeared in the security market as a result of an inversion of door keys usage: *key that cannot open the door* generated the idea of keys that can open the door only if the door is not locked with two turns of the key. This allows giving keys to people who clean the house and allowing them to enter only during the week, for example. During the weekends the door is locked with two turns and only the owner can open it.

8.4.4 *Elimination*

Elimination consists of removing one/ several element(s) of the product or service.

Tangible Product or Service   A stock market purchase order *that does not happen* led to a brilliant new service. This service has been offered to business schools in order to train students and make online simulations.

The elimination of moderators, locations, and scripts in qualitative research has led to the recent trend of *ethnographic surveys*. They consist of marketers spending one whole day as part of the target group. The fact of spending a whole day makes consumers finally act as they really are and give honest opinions.

A *telephone without a cable* joining the receiver to the telephone led to the idea of wireless telephones, ideal for moving around the house or outside in the garden when talking on the phone.

A *car without one wheel* has led to the idea of a motorbike of three wheels developed by Aprilia (Los Angeles 500 Model). Riders do not fall off, because they are more stable.

Packaging   *Home ambience perfume without a bottle* could be solved through perfumed wax that gives a good smell to a room. The perfume flows naturally from the wax without needing a container. This helps constantly perfume the room.

Brand Attributes   *Brand without attributes* led to the idea of generic brands. It also applies to a private label brand (PLB) that belongs to a distributor such as a supermarket or clothing store). These brands have no image separate from the distributor and tend to be cheaper.

Eliminating space between cars led to the idea of parking garages with cars automatically parked, so space is completely filled.

Usage or Purchase   A *motorbike that cannot be parked* has led Honda to develop the Honda Caixa: a small city motorbike that can be folded in a box 17 cm. by 80 cm. (7 inches by 32 inches). People can keep the vehicle inside their apartments.

In the business-to-business market, the elimination of one step of the purchase process, *transport for delivering*, led to the idea of industrial clusters—all customers and suppliers of the same industry being in the same industrial area.

The elimination of *taking photos to develop* led to the Polaroid's idea by which photos are developed instantly.

The removal of the act of flushing a toilet led to the idea in public restrooms of placing a photoelectric cell that detects when the user has left. Then, water flows automatically.

8.4.5 Exaggeration

Exaggeration consists of exaggerating upward or downward one/several element(s) of the product or service. It also consists of imagining a perfect product or service.

Tangible Product or Service A bicycle for *two or three riders* led to the idea of tandems, the most rented bicycle in the world.

Lacoste *increased the length* of its popular shirts and found out that they could be sold as summer cover-ups for women to wear over their swimsuits.

In amusement parks, the following exaggeration was proposed: *terror castle with real monsters*. This led to the idea of placing actors and actresses performing as characters of successful terror films. Some parks that had problems attracting local visitors now experienced a substantial increase of sales with the new terror castle.

The exaggeration of *recording the programs of one week and watching them without ads* led to a concept under development by Tech Foundries: INOUT TV. It would consist of hardware with capacity to store up to 80 hours of TV. The system would allow selecting a whole week of programs to be recorded. Programs would be digitally stored and ads would be automatically eliminated.

Packaging The exaggeration of *water bottles of 50 liters* yielded the idea of using them as water fountains in the middle of offices, by placing them on stands that have plastic taps.

Brand Attributes A *car as small as possible* was the downward exaggeration that led Mercedes-Benz to develop Smart, a new category in the car market.

An exaggeration of the deodorant attribute "perfumed" was converted into the concept: *deodorant that always produces smell.* Unilever created Axe, a perfumed deodorant that opened a new subcategory, perfumed deodorants for males.

An exaggeration of the attribute "duration" of a lottery number led to the idea of offering the following service: someone buying a lottery number is asked how many weeks he wants it to be valid. You pay for as many weeks you want it to be valid. The incremental volume is substantial.

An upwards exaggeration of a *cartoon film duration* (five minutes) led Walt Disney to create the first full-length animated film, *Snow White.* Critics said that Disney was crazy. Instead, he created a film with moments of sadness, joy, persecution, songs, dancing, love—and gags). A new category in cinema industry was born.

169

Usage or Purchase The exaggeration of saying *contact lenses that are changed every day* was the source of disposable lenses, now available in all contact lens brands. They last for approximately one week, and losing them does not create a crisis anymore.

Imagining a toilet so perfect that it calculates the water needed led to a toilet with two levers: one for using the whole capacity of the tank and another for using only half. An important amount of water is saved each month.

8.4.6   Reordering

Reordering consists of changing the order or sequence of one/several element(s) of the product or service.

Tangible Product or Service *People request ads to be sent to them.* This inversion led to the recent concept of permission marketing offered through the Internet. People interested in receiving particular ads receive them by e-mail. They are rewarded with points or money. This service was complemented with the sending of surveys or ad tests.

Rum mixed with juices before opening the bottle led Bacardi to create Bacardi Breezers, a low-proof beverage with low alcohol content and already mixed with citric flavoring. This product belongs to the ready to drink (RTD) category, which was born as a result of this lateral marketing displacement.

Packaging   *Popcorn packed before being popped* led to the idea of microwave popcorn. The corn kernals are put inside a paper bag, which is placed inside the microwave. The heat inflates the bag and causes the corn to pop. This allows people to eat freshly made hot popcorn without using a pan.

Brand Attributes   Reordering attributes can be done by giving priority to a secondary attribute.[7] The Audi coupe concept was, "There are faster coupes than Audi, but Audi is the most comfortable one": *comfortable before faster* in a coupe!

Usage or Purchase   The idea of a *shaving lotion for use before shaving* led Williams to create Lectric Shave, a lotion that when applied to the beard before shaving dries it and allows for easier shaving.

   Obtaining foam from a soap before using it led to the idea of putting foam inside dispensers in public rest rooms. The hand is quickly filled with foam and the volume of soap usage is lowered considerably, with consequent savings.

8.5   Connecting a Possible Market with the New Product

At this point, we will have a new product or service idea that may or may not make sense at all.

---

[7]Reordering attributes tends to create subcategories rather than innovations, since the only thing that changes is the importance of the attributes and, therefore, is in most cases a new positioning in the same market.

Any of the three techniques described in Chapter 6 could be used: finding a possible setting, extracting the positive, or imagining the purchase process step-by-step.

8.5.1 Finding a Possible Setting

For example, a paper carton container was thought to be preferable to glass or plastic for use *inside boats* for better and safer storing. Afterward, the paper carton moved into *home usage*.

The idea of a 50-liter bottle of water was made valid by finding a useful place for storing water: *inside offices*.

The men's ties with characters such as Donald Duck, Mickey Mouse, or Bugs Bunny were thought valid for *certain people* who may like to show themselves as "happy" and "optimistic" people.

A too-small car finds a setting in *urban areas* where parking space is scarce. In other settings, Smart may not be as useful.

8.5.2 Extracting the Positive Things

The good thing about changing contact lenses every day is that it *would not be a problem in losing one*. Disposable lenses also would be easier to use when practicing sports or swimming.

Microwave popcorn makes it *unnecessary to use a pan*, butter, or oil. It is clean, easy, and fast.

A two–person cycle is not too comfortable and requires going to the same place. The positive thing is that *it is funny* and allows riders to share good moments. These are the reasons why it is rented in tourist places. Almost no one buys them for their own use.

8.5.3 *Imagining the Purchase Process*

A *motorbike that cannot be parked* forces us to imagine how we could fold it. This was accomplished by Honda engineers who managed to "pack" the motorbike.

Lottery with no raffle obliges us to think about how to communicate the winner to the person. The connection was made by imagining the buyer knowing the result instantly.

The *telephone without cable* connection was made by trying to make sound waves arrive some way to the receiver.

8.6 The Product May Need to Be Adjusted

When considering connecting a product to a possible market, we may have to make some additional changes to it.

The carton container was possible only if it had a different shape (a block). Smart had to be positioned as trendy, in order to justify paying for a car to carry only two passengers. Prepacked popcorn had to be cooked in a microwave in order to make the product possible. The office water fountains required adding a stand and a plastic tap to the bottle.

8.7 A Complete Case: The Double-Decker Car

Here we want to introduce an example of a lateral marketing innovation at the product level that does not exist. We use the car market and apply the technique of combination.

We will combine cars with London buses, which are known for having two floors. The resulting concept would be a two-story vehicle.

Let's extract the positive things: ideal for families of many members. If the vehicle is not stable enough, the upper deck should be made less high. If still dangerous, the upper deck could be the steering section of the car and the lower deck could be used for passengers, allowing more people capacity to the same wagon.

There exist two-story buses. Why not cars? A possible name for the category: Wagon-Two.

Lateral Marketing at the Marketing Mix Level

T his chapter gives practical recommendations on how to apply lateral marketing at the marketing mix level.

9.1 Effects of Lateral Marketing at the Mix Level

Making a lateral displacement using as a focus the rest of the marketing mix elements (price, place, and promotion) implies moving away from the current way of presenting the product or service to the customer. But we are not modifying the essence of the product or service, nor the need, target, or situation that our product or service covers.

In most cases, the lateral marketing displacement made at the mix level will result in a subcategory or an innovative commercial formula for the product or service, rather than a completely new business or category. Its application leads to outcomes that may converge with the ones of vertical marketing.

Applying lateral marketing at the marketing mix level will lead to moving inside our category with innovative distribution, pricing, or communication formulas without altering the product or service.

The strength of using the marketing mix as a focus for generating displacements is its immediate application. Original new concepts and products need time to be developed. In contrast, the outcome of lateral marketing applied at the mix level is more tactical and short-term oriented, giving some immediate ideas.

When we apply lateral marketing at the mix level we may have two different objectives:

1. Applying alternative marketing mix strategies for our product or service.

2. Finding new marketing mix formulas.

For covering the first objective, we propose to concentrate efforts on one technique: substitution. This operation gives very successful results and is very easy to apply. We can call this technique "taking the mix of other products." The other five methods are better for creating new pricing, distribution, or communication formulas and will be treated separately.

9.2 Lateral Marketing for Diversifying Our Marketing Mix: "Taking the Mix of Other Products"

> *"Taking the mix of other products" consists of applying* existing pricing, distribution or communication formulas *that correspond to other existing products or services and which are not naturally associated with the category we compete in.*

Let's see some examples:

9.2.1 Pricing

Coffee vending machine companies have applied the credit card concept to selling coffee. One inserts the card into a machine along with as many coins as he/she wants. Credit is accumulated into the card and can be spent at any time. *Marketing mix innovation: selling coffee with a prepaid card system.*

In Portugal, people use ATMs very extensively. ATMs are normally used for withdrawing cash. Energy companies, such as electricity, gas, or water, charge bills through ATMs, rather than mailing them to customers' home addresses. *Marketing mix innovation: payment of bills through ATMs.*

The Tele-Tac company has developed a system for charging highway tolls through the car owner's bank account. The system consists of an electronic device in the toll barrier that is able to read a card installed in the car's front window. A computer stores the day, hour, and car license plate and bills the driver each month. *Marketing mix innovation: charging highway tolls to the bank account.*

Multinational large advertisers are starting to pay their advertising agencies in relation to sales increases obtained after campaigns. *Marketing mix innovation: agency fees calculated as sales agent commissions.*

Some Internet stock market agents now charge a fixed price per purchase or sale rather than a percentage price. *Marketing mix innovation: transactions charged on a fixed price basis.*

Supermarkets have converted regular discount promotions into innovative pricing policies: "points rewards systems." Points are converted into a cash check sent by the chain at the end of the month. This is a creative formula for postponing the discount and creating customer loyalty at the same time. *Marketing mix innovation: rewards concept tied to regular household shopping.*

Innovative restaurants have appeared that don't charge per dish, but charge $6 for entering. The customer is allowed to eat as much as he/she wants of salads, pasta, and pizza. *Marketing mix innovation: flat rates for variable quantities eaten.*

A company gives away a little machine into which tablets must be placed to kill insects. The machine works only when a tablet is inserted. *Marketing mix innovation: a pricing policy imitating the one used by razor blade companies—giving away the razor and making money on the blades.*

Observe that in all these examples the payment system was not a new one. The innovation came from taking an existing payment formula and applying it to a product or service that didn't use that pricing formula.

9.2.2 Distribution

Real estate companies have started to sell houses and apartments by setting up shops in the middle of urban commercial areas, instead of advertising in newspapers and using agents for selling. *Marketing mix innovation: selling houses in shops.*

Logistics companies are selling last-minute transports by

sending e-mails to regular customers and communicating empty capacity of their trucks in certain routes. *Marketing mix innovation: selling logistics by e-mail.*

Victoria's Secret created a new distribution concept by displaying lingerie that customers could see and touch next to fashionable clothing. *Marketing mix innovation: selling lingerie as fashion.*

Placing condoms in vending machines allowed distributing them through discos. *Marketing mix innovation: selling condoms in vending machines.*

Selling bread in exclusive shops led to the creation of innovative bakery distribution concepts under the franchising form. *Marketing mix innovation: selling bread in exclusive outlets.*

Selling books through the Internet is Amazon's breakthrough business concept.

Selling airplane tickets over the phone or the Internet and bypassing travel agencies was Virgin Airlines' strategy. *Marketing mix innovation: selling airplane tickets over the phone or Internet.*

Car dealers buy your used car in order to sell you a new one. An accumulation of used cars stock has been experienced by many auto dealers. The new idea was to sell used cars using the distribution formula of giant retailers: an exposition area of several thousand square yards with hundreds of used cars available. *Marketing mix innovation: selling cars like Ikea sells furniture.*

Eismann is a German company that decided to sell and distribute frozen food in the same way as encyclopedias: door-to-door sales through sales agents who receive a commission.

Marketing mix innovation: selling food using the encyclopedia distribution formula.

Again, note that in all these examples the distribution formula was not a new one. The innovation came from taking an existing distribution or sales system and applying it to a product or service that had not formerly used it.

9.2.3   Communication

Telecom companies have found more efficient and profitable media and small enterprise prospects through placing ads on TV prime time programs. By offering *business-to-business services on TV*, they reached more small business prospects.

Some companies are inserting CDs with their ads and product descriptions *inside magazines*, instead of distributing them through regular TV broadcasts.

A company that sold high-quality and exclusive family tombs organized *group visits to the cemetery* as their main communication activity.

The successful message of Lee Iacocca that boosted Chrysler sales—*"If you think there is a better car than Chrysler, buy it"*—was used in other countries by other brands. In Spain, for example, the same message was given by the general manager of a detergent company! It was really successful and is still recalled.

A challenge would be to *advertise food using catalogs*. Eismann, the German frozen food manufacturer, uses this communication medium.

A Portuguese courier company discovered through market research that it had the image of always being late in early morning deliveries. It decided to have its branded vans and cars circulate in Lisbon streets between six and nine in the morning. *Marketing mix innovation: a courier company advertising through its vans*.

Trident gum uses endorsers for promoting its sugarless chewing gum: dentists. *Dentists endorsing chewing gums!* This campaign was a real success and boosted the brand's sales.

9.3 Lateral Marketing for Finding New Marketing Mix Formulas: The Rest of the Lateral Displacements

The rest of lateral displacement techniques are useful in order to come up with:

- New pricing, distribution, or communication strategies.
- Concrete innovative marketing mix actions.

Both types of cases are discussed next for the five remaining lateral displacement techniques.

9.3.1 Combination

The combination of "phone" + "internet" has led many companies to create communication and direct sales channels using the Internet and telephone as the way to purchase—for example, booking theater tickets.

The combination of "TV" + "telephone" + "sending by mail" has led to the Tele-shop channel, with late-night programs selling products that are difficult to find in any shop.

The combination of "expensive" + "strong discount" has created the strategy of setting an expensive price and communicating short-term continuous sales promotions of 50 percent off. This strategy is very efficient in products such as carpets and other decorative goods, where turnover is low.

9.3.2 Inversion

The inversion "shops own the wholesaler" led to the idea of cooperatives, which appeared in the 1960s and 1970s.

The inversion "shops pay to customers" led to the business of pawnshops and "cash converters." These shops either buy your product outright or buy on consignment.

"No message as a message" has been the strategy of a financial advisory company whose ad was a silent ad. The implicit message was: confidentiality.

9.3.3 Elimination

Eliminating channels led to the direct distribution concept, using mail, phone, or other means of distribution.

Elimination of employees has led to many self-service distribution formulas, applicable not only in restaurants and gas stations, but also in clothing and other stores.

Saab is a brand addressed to people with a discrete lifestyle: people who like to own a high-quality car, but do not want to show off or appear luxurious. The strategy of Saab was to do little advertising: by reducing the promotion intensity, the brand appeared more discrete.

The operation "a shop that does not sell" has led an important multinational of bathroom furniture to create showrooms displaying their products, but you cannot buy them there. If interested, you are given the addresses of authorized distributors.

9.3.4 Exaggeration

The exaggeration "We want to be in every single selling point" leads to the intensive distribution strategy followed by Coca-Cola and other major brands.

The exaggeration: "We want to talk to all our potential customers" led Tupper Ware to its well-known communication and distribution strategy: organized meetings/parties in homes.

Exaggerating the message: "We want to show the biggest metal object that could be painted in blue" led Pepsi to paint a Concorde blue as a way of presenting the new Pepsi can design. The day after the presentation, the blue Concorde was featured in all media (TV, newspapers, etc.) This type of communication strategy (huge events) has been widely used.

9.3.5 Reordering

An advertising agency knew that leaflet mailings were thrown away by marketing managers and directors. The reordering "throw the leaflet into the basket before opening the letter" led to the idea of sending a basket to marketing managers with a creased paper inside. The message was: "We saved you the effort of throwing our leaflet away; we already did it for you." All managers took the paper and looked inside the leaflet to know what was being advertised.

Advertising after selling has led many construction companies to put a plaque saying "constructed by. . . . " There is no better advertising than communicating what you already sold!

January sales promotions before Christmas was a strategy used by an important European clothing distribution company. It is now famous for starting after-Christmas sales some days before Christmas.

9.4   The Product May Need to Be Adjusted

Depending on the lateral displacement, in some cases we may have to do minor adaptations to the product or market.

For example, condoms in vending machines implies selling one- or two-unit packs, which are rarely seen in pharmacies.

Selling houses through shops implied taking photos of all houses and apartments for sale. This was not normally done before: A simple text appeared in newspapers, and visits were arranged when potential customers phoned.

Tele-Tac required placing expensive machines in toll barriers and distributing special cards to car owners, which had to be placed in the front windows of cars.

Victoria's Secret's concept required a special effort at cloth designs and communication in order to build up a fashionable brand image.

9.5   A Complete Case: Steel Shops

We wanted to introduce a possible nonexisting idea in order to illustrate the method in this chapter.

The idea of "selling steel in shops" could lead to the idea of a steel manufacturer creating shops where the staff can explain the different applications of the product: car bodies, window structures, or others that might interest end customers.

By helping end consumers know the steel brand and feel confident, car manufacturers might be willing to communicate the steel brand they use as an additional selling argument for their products.

This may recall the strategy of car seat brands Recaro or ABS. These brands compete in the business-to-business market (selling to car manufacturers). But by building up an end-consumer brand image, car manufacturers can use both brands as selling arguments for their high-quality models.

Implementing
Lateral Marketing

B efore we move on to the implementation strategy for lateral marketing, let's recap what we have learned:

- Companies need to innovate if they are to grow and prosper.
- An excessively high percentage of new products fail (80 percent in consumer goods and 40 percent in business goods) in spite of careful market research and planning. The reasons for the crisis in innovation must be examined. One reason is the traditional process for innovation.
- Most of these new products involve offering a more specialized version of something to the same market, such as a new flavor, size, packaging, and so on. The source of this strategy is segmentation or *vertical thinking*.
- The repeated application of vertical thinking results in creating a hyperfragmented market; in this scenario few segments or niches remain that are big enough to yield profit.

- Marketers need a complementary way of thinking up new products and services that will lead to new categories or new markets. The resulting innovations will have a greater chance of profit, although the risk may be greater as well. The source for this strategy is *lateral thinking*.

- Lateral marketing thinking uses a distinct framework and processes that can be taught to anyone and can become a part of an innovative company's culture along with vertical marketing thinking.

Lateral marketing thinking might occur spontaneously within an individual and within any kind of company. The existence of McDonald's in and of itself is an example of putting together of the ideas of "food" + "fast." A new market was created as a result. Another example is a recent innovation at Sprint subsequently copied by others. The company has developed a new phone that resulted from putting together the ideas of "cellular phone" + "camera."

If lateral thinking was diffused throughout companies as an idea-generating and a problem-solving approach, they would be transformed into more innovative market creators. The reality is that this will happen only in companies that specifically reach for that bigger vision, namely to become an innovative company like Sony or 3M.

When we speak of innovation here we are not limiting the concept to merely the thinking up of new products. Innovation includes developing new processes, new channels, and new business concepts. There are manifold possibilities.

192

10.1   The Three Systems of an Innovative Company: The Gary Hamel Model

An innovative company is not one filled with a few wildly creative individuals who spontaneously think up new ideas. Rather it is characterized by several systems that have been installed and perfected over time. Gary Hamel[1] suggested that an innovative company would operate three systems: an idea market, a capital market, and a talent market.

10.1.1   An Idea Market

An idea market means that the company has established a system for actively soliciting, collecting, and evaluating new ideas. The company appoints a high-level executive to manage an idea development, collection, and evaluation (IDCE) system. This executive meets with an idea committee consisting of high-level representatives from different departments. The committee meets bimonthly and evaluates ideas that have flowed in from company employees and company partners such as suppliers, distributors, and dealers. The committee arranges funding for evaluating the more attractive ideas to test their worth.

When Walt Disney was producing his first full-length animated film (*Snow White and the Seven Dwarfs*) he asked all his employees to come up with jokes for the film. Every good idea

---

[1]See Gary Hamel, "Bringing Silicon Valley Inside," *Harvard Business Review* (September 1999).

would receive some dollars as an incentive. The reward generated truly innovative thinking.

Dave Packard received a brilliant idea from an employee when he was having lunch in the office. He became so excited that he gave the only thing he had in his hands at that moment to the employee: a banana. Since then, every good idea was rewarded with a golden banana! Receiving one was a sign of distinction in the company.

Many companies organize brainstorming sessions or off-site meetings to generate ideas. Admittedly, brainstorming sessions are a productive system for generating ideas. But assuming that needed ideas can be produced at a concrete time and place is not enough for building an idea market.

Imagine that we placed Albert Einstein in a hotel room and asked him to find the theory of relativity by next Tuesday. It is absurd. The task of creating marketing innovations cannot have a concrete day, hour, and place. Idea generation should be a regular activity in any marketing department and throughout a company.

The reason why meetings for finding new ideas are not a regular activity of many companies' marketing departments is the lack of a method. Brainstorming sessions are conducted as a way of letting imagination flow and proposing as many crazy ideas as possible. But many managers do not like brainstorming sessions because the final outcome is not always clear and a method is lacking.

The lateral marketing framework should overcome this problem. Now, the objective is not *to propose ideas without order*, but *to connect proposals that arise through concrete and shared displacement techniques*. The marketing manager says:

"What do you think about the following lateral displacement? Should we dedicate time on how to connect it?" All colleagues will understand this as setting in motion a lateral marketing work process.

The lateral marketing framework will make idea generation a normal activity within the marketing department. Asking marketers to apply the lateral marketing process will ensure obtaining a good bank of ideas for feeding the idea market.

10.1.2   A Capital Market

Funding must be set aside to support researching the ultimate worth of initially attractive ideas. One idea might receive $50,000 to support focus group research; another idea might require $200,000 to test whether a new type of disk drive can be made. The dollar amount should be relative to the idea.

Part of the funds should be destined not only to researching the potential of the new ideas, but also to engage the staff in thinking laterally. Seminars or training courses for applying lateral marketing should also be funded. Marketers need to learn to work together with this new framework, embracing it and making it systematic.

10.1.3   A Talent Market

The firm will need to have or hire people with the necessary talents to develop the best ideas. The firm needs to tap the talent of marketing researchers, electronic engineers, or other skilled implementers.

Talent is also necessary to *connect lateral displacements*. We would propose the following:

The first part of the lateral marketing process, "doing a lateral displacement," could be done individually. One only needs to select one of the three levels and apply any or several of the six techniques described in this book. Some displacements will already be discarded individually and others may be assessed as potential, so this person may decide to show only the potential ideas.

A *lateral marketing meeting* should be dedicated to listening to displacements and thinking about possible ways to connect them. The meeting is a working session where a group applies analytical and vertical thinking. Remember that "doing connections" requires applying logic with more strength than ever.

The contrast with brainstorming is radical. In brainstorming sessions, the objective is to generate displacements through canceling judgment. In a lateral marketing meeting, however, the time is dedicated to thinking about the usefulness and possibilities of displacements made by others. Therefore, the feeling of wasting time is eliminated and these sessions can be more regularly scheduled.

The question now arises: what to do with the discarded versus the valid ideas. Here are two proposals:

What to Do with the Discarded Ideas: Recycle Them! Once, when Edison was working on light filaments and had discarded thousands of experiments, an assistant asked how he managed to persist despite "failures." Edison replied that he did not understand the question—there had not been any failures. On the contrary, he had discovered thousands of systems that should not be considered anymore."[2]

Nothing can be more true. There are three reasons to keep the discarded ideas:

1. The first reason is that storing discarded displacements allows selecting other techniques and levels not used yet. If we know that the idea of inverting the packaging has already been made, we might try another technique or another product element.

2. The second reason is that we must avoid repeating the thinking process of trying to connect a given displacement. If, for example, after some hours of meetings we finally discard the idea of the double-decker car, we should not tie up time and resources again soon. It is akin to understanding and studying history so as to avoid repeating it.

3. The third reason is that the company's market or position might change or new marketing staff might find valid connections. The storage of the discarded ideas can be sources of inspiration for other professionals.

So, we recommend keeping discarded ideas. There may be a chance to recycle them!

Storage of Lateral Marketing Displacements and Connections: A Well-Structured Archive of Ideas   The lateral marketing

---

[2]Michael Michalko, *Cracking Creativity: The Secrets of Creative Genius* (Berkeley, CA: Ten Speed Press, 1998).

framework allows a structured system for archiving ideas. Ideas can be stored following the structure proposed in this book:

1. Lateral displacements of market:
   1.1. Already connected.
   1.2. Connection pending.
   1.3. Discarded but filed.
2. Lateral displacements of product:
   2.1. Already connected.
   2.2. Connection pending.
   2.3. Discarded but filed.
3. Lateral displacements of marketing mix:
   3.1. Already connected.
   3.2. Connection pending.
   3.3. Discarded but filed.

All this material can be stored in a computer folder file so that any professional can check ideas that are already implemented, pending, or temporarily rejected. The file becomes an asset of innovative thinking and therefore intellectual capital.

Observe the importance of implementing this archive. Marketing professionals can take any idea generated in the past and reexamine its potential. The archive also helps them avoid spending precious time and resources on dead-end ideas.

10.2   Next Step: Managing the Whole Process

Beyond these three markets, the company needs a new product development process with a set of clear gates to let good ideas pass all the way to fruition and launch, or to stop bad ideas from going further as early as possible. The normal stages of the new product development process are:

1. Idea development.
2. Concept development.
3. Concept testing.
4. Financial analysis.
5. Prototype development.
6. Prototype testing.
7. Market testing.
8. Market launch.

Valid ideas are potential new concepts, markets, or categories. What to do with them depends on the risks associated with their implementation. The higher the risk, the more effort should be placed on testing the idea.

Best practices in carrying out each step are well described in textbooks.[3] Suffice it to say that lateral marketing as well as vertical marketing serve the purpose of helping the company

---

[3]See Philip Kotler, *Marketing Management*, 11th edition (Upper Saddle River, NJ: Prentice Hall, 2003).

get to the first two stages in this eight-step process. Nothing happens in a company until there are ideas.

The need has never been more urgent for finding ways to create new ideas. Products and services are being treated as commodities in most markets. Competitors can rapidly spot and copy new ideas. No firm can ever afford to rest. Only firms that engage in continuous creativity and innovation have a chance to secure a profitable future.

Quick Reminder of the Lateral Marketing Framework

Choose a product or service.

- The one currently marketed, for innovating while growing.
- A competitor, for finding a substitute.

Step 1: Select one level of the vertical marketing process.

- Market level.
- Product level.
- Rest of the marketing mix level.

Step 2: Make a lateral displacement. See techniques for each previous level.

- Market level: Change one dimension.

    Need or utility.

    Target.

  Time.

  Place.

  Situation.

  Experience.

- Product level: apply to a product element (tangible product, packaging, brand attributes, usage or purchase) one of the six techniques:

  Substitution.

  Combination.

  Inversion.

  Elimination.

  Exaggeration.

  Reordering.

- Rest of the marketing mix level. Apply the commercial formulas of other categories.

  The pricing formulas of other categories.

  The distribution formulas of other categories.

  The communication formulas of other categories.

Step 3: Solve the gap by applying a valuation technique.

- Imagine the purchase process.
- Extract the positive.
- Find a setting.

INDEX

Index

Index